Library of Medieval Women

Mechthild of Magdeburg:
Selections from *The Flowing Light of the Godhead*

T0341528

Library of Medieval Women

ISSN 1369–9652

Series Editor: Jane Chance

The Library of Medieval Women aims to make available, in an English translation, significant works by, for, and about medieval women, from the age of the Church Fathers to the sixteenth century. The series encompasses many forms of writing, from poetry, visions, biography and autobiography, and letters to sermons, treatises and encyclopedias; the subject matter is equally diverse: theology and mysticism, classical mythology, medicine and science, history, hagiography, and instructions for anchoresses. Each text is presented with an introduction setting the material in context and a guide to further reading.

We welcome suggestions for future titles in the series. Proposals or queries may be sent directly to the editor or publisher at the addresses given below; all submissions will receive prompt and informed consideration.

Professor Jane Chance. E-mail: jchance@rice.edu

Boydell & Brewer Limited, PO Box 9, Woodbridge, Suffolk, IP12 3DF, UK. E-mail: boydell@boydell.co.uk. Website: www.boydell.co.uk

Mechthild of Magdeburg:
Selections from *The Flowing Light of the Godhead*

Translated from the Middle High German with Introduction, Notes and Interpretive Essay

Elizabeth A. Andersen

University of Newcastle

D.S. BREWER

First published 2003
D. S. Brewer, Cambridge

Reprinted in paperback and transferred to digital printing 2012

ISBN 978–0–85991–786–5 hardback
ISBN 978–1–84384–297–2 paperback

D. S. Brewer is an imprint of Boydell & Brewer Ltd
PO Box 9, Woodbridge, Suffolk IP12 3DF, UK
and of Boydell & Brewer Inc.
668 Mount Hope Ave, Rochester, NY 14620-2731, USA
website: www.boydellandbrewer.com

A CIP catalogue record for this book is available
from the British Library

Library of Congress Catalog Card Number 2003004454

This publication is printed on acid-free paper

Contents

In memory of my mother

Introduction

Mechthild of Magdeburg's sole book, *Das fließende Licht der Gottheit* ['*The Flowing Light of the Godhead*'],[1] written between *c*. 1250 and *c*. 1282, deserves to be more widely known in the English-speaking world for a number of reasons. First and foremost, it is an outstanding piece of imaginative writing in its documentation of the author's relationship with God and with her contemporaries. Secondly, within the context of German literary history the *FL* is the first text in the tradition of mystical writing that was neither a translation nor a free adaptation of a Latin text, but rather an independent composition in the vernacular. Thirdly, this text was written by a woman and thus offers insights into the cultural and social-historical context of the female religious in thirteenth century Europe.[2]

Manuscript transmission, editing and translation

Mechthild's original Low German text has not survived; her writings reach the modern reader through the filter of a mid-fourteenth century translation into the Alemannic dialect of Middle High German. Heinrich of Nördlingen, a secular priest, was responsible for this transposition of Mechthild's writings into High German. He served as confessor and spiritual advisor in Cistercian and Dominican convents near Basle and was at the centre of a group of people known as 'Gottesfreunde' ['friends of God'] whom he sought to support in their striving towards greater spiritual knowledge and achievement. The Middle High German version of the *FL* is fully extant in only one manuscript, E (Ms 277), which is part of a codex held in the library of the Benedictine monastery at Einsiedeln in the canton of Schwyz in Switzerland.[3] First evidence of the reception of

---

1   From here on the abbreviation *FL* is used to refer to *Das fließende Licht der Gottheit*.
2   For a fuller and more comprehensive account of what follows see Andersen (2000: 11–146).
3   E is a 'collected manuscript' [*Sammelhandschrift*] comprising two parts. Part 1 contains the *FL* and two short pieces of mystical writing and Part 2 sermons by

Mechthild's work is to be found in the *Lux divinitatis* [The light of the divinity],[4] a translation into Latin of the first six of the seven books of the *FL* by Dominicans from Halle that was completed by the end of the thirteenth century. The earlier of the two extant manuscripts, Rb, is also from the mid-fourteenth century, and, again like the vernacular E, was produced in the southwest of the German-speaking world, in the vicinity of Basle. The translators generally adhered fairly closely to Mechthild's text, but there is evidence of editing in the toning down of passages where the expression is explicitly erotic and where the thought might have been construed as heretical.[5] Furthermore, the material has been radically re-ordered. In the *FL* it would seem that the passages occur, broadly speaking, in chronological sequence, whereas in the *Ld* they are grouped according to theme.

Mechthild's book was first made accessible to the modern world in 1869 in an edition produced by Pater Gall Morel, who was the librarian of the monastery at Einsiedeln. Just eight years later, an edition of the *Ld*, based on both extant manuscripts, was produced by the Benedictine monks of Solesmes in northeastern France.[6] Morel's somewhat flawed edition was eventually replaced in 1990 by Hans Neumann's thorough reworking of the text, followed by an accompanying volume of textual notes and studies in 1993. The benefits of Neumann's scholarship were extended to a greater German readership by Margot Schmidt's revision of her original translation of 1955 based on Morel's edition. In the English-speaking world, the translations of Lucy Menzies (1953) and Christiane Mesch-Galvani (1991), both based on Morel's edition, were superseded in 1998 by Frank Tobin's translation of Neumann's edition. This translation has the additional benefit of having been executed in dialogue with Schmidt's revised German translation.

Meister Eckhart, treatises on mystical topics attributed to him and a series of queries and sentences. For a description of E see Neumann (1993: 175ff.). There are three other manuscripts which contain significant portions of Mechthild's book: C – Colmar, from the first half of the fifteenth century, W – Würzburg, from the end of the fourteenth century and B – Budapest, from 1416. For details of these and other fragments see Vollman-Profe (in Neumann, 1990: XIff.).

4   From here on the abbreviation *Ld* is used to refer to the *Lux divinitatis*.

5   Cf. Becker (1951: 38).

6   The editor, Dom Louis Paquelin, completed the thirteenth century *Ld* by rendering Book VII into Latin himself. References to the *Ld* are given according to the page and line of the Solesmes edition (1877), e.g. *Ld*: 436, 20–4.

Biography of Mechthild

Chronology, social background and education

We know nothing about Mechthild other than what can be gleaned from her writings and the editing of these by contemporaries. Hans Neumann's (1954/64) reconstruction of significant junctures in Mechthild's life through his painstaking analysis of her text is still generally accepted, at least in outline. According to Neumann, Mechthild was born in the vicinity of Magdeburg in *c.* 1207, left her parental home in *c.* 1230 to live as a beguine in Magdeburg, started to write down her experiences in *c.* 1250 and composed Books I–V between *c.* 1250 and *c.* 1259 and Book VI in the following decade. She entered the convent of St Mary at Helfta in Saxony in *c.* 1270, composing her seventh and final book there before her death in *c.* 1282.[7] However, Neumann's putative chronology has been subsequently compromised by a greater awareness of the formative influence of hagiographical literature on Mechthild's self-projection. Thus the 'autobiographical' account of her spiritual development, which Mechthild gives in IV, 2, is expressed in conventional hagiographical paradigms:[8] the innocence of the child, the early religious experience, the voluntary renunciation of a pleasant life in the parental home, the estrangement from family and friends, the withdrawal from the world.[9]

Mechthild informs her reader that she can read and, more interestingly, that she can write,[10] but asserts that she is unversed in Latin.[11] The level of her education would indicate that, at the very least, she was born into a wealthy family. Neumann suggests that Mechthild was from a 'ritterliche Burgmannenfamilie' [knightly family owing garrison duty].[12] The service rendered by the 'Burgmann' as vassal to

---

7   Schmidt (1995: 397, n. 292) proposes *c.* 1294 as an alternative date for Mechthild's death. Neumann's conjecture has, however, won greater currency. Cf. Andersen (2000: 45).

8   References to passages in Mechthild's text are cited according to the book in which they occur and then according to the number of the chapter in the book. Thus IV, 2 is Book IV, chapter 2. Where I wish to draw attention to particular sections in a passage that I have translated, I have included a page reference, e.g. IV, 2 [p. xx]. References to passages not translated in this selection are cited in accordance with the Neumann edition, that is with the addition of line references, e.g. IV, 2, 25–27.

9   Cf. Peters (1988: 55).

10 Cf. II, 26 [p. 47], III, 1 [p. 56], V, 32 [p. 99]. Cf. also VI, 43, 2–5.

11 Cf. II, 3, 48–50.

12 Neumann (1987: 260).

his lord, the 'Burggraf', often opened the way into the ranks of the lesser nobility.[13] It is evident from her writings that Mechthild was well acquainted with the Bible, in particular the Psalms, the Song of Songs, the Gospels and Revelation, with methods of biblical exegesis and the liturgy. As Mechthild had not benefited from the Latin-based theological education of the convent, she would not have had immediate knowledge of theological texts in Latin. Nonetheless, the influence of the following has been detected in her writings: Augustine, Bernard of Clairvaux, Hugh and Richard of St. Victor, Pseudo-Dionysius and Joachim of Fiore.[14] These sources of influence could have been mediated to her through sermons and instruction by the Dominicans in whose pastoral care she seems to have been, as witnessed by the preface to the *FL*: '[Mechthild] followed faithfully and perfectly the light and the teaching of the Order of Preachers.'[15] From early in the history of Mechthild scholarship, reference has been frequently made to Mechthild's evident acquaintance with courtly culture.[16]

There are many echoes of secular love poetry, both in imagery and form, in Mechthild's descriptions of nuptial mysticism. However, there is no less evidence for the strong influence of native folk song.[17] Furthermore, Mechthild also drew creatively on aspects of everyday living and folk oral tradition, incorporating, for example, features from gnomic sayings and drinking songs.[18]

Life as a beguine
In the Latin preface to the *FL* Mechthild is identified as a beguine[19] and on one occasion in her writings she specifically identifies herself as such: 'O you very foolish beguines [. . .] Now I, who am the least amongst you, [. . .]' (III, 15 [p. 61]). Beguines were women who chose to lead a life of voluntary poverty, chastity and religious devo-

---

13   There is no fixed term in English for 'Burgmann'. 'Burggraf' is best rendered as 'castellan'.
14   Cf. Neumann (1987: 264), Ruh (1993: 285ff.) and Schmidt (1995: xxxviii ff.).
15   There is a short preface in Latin to Mechthild's text in the Einsiedeln manuscript, which is followed by an *Index rerum*, a list of selected main themes treated in Books I–V. This Latin preface, but not the table of contents, is immediately followed by a translation of it in Middle High German.
16   Cf. Lüers (1926/66: 35f.).
17   Mohr (1963: 394).
18   Hellgardt (1996).
19   'Liber iste fuit teutonico cuidam begine . . . inspiratus' ['this book was revealed in German to a certain beguine'].

tion while remaining in the secular world. Unlike nuns, they did not take a vow of obedience, nor did they take a vow of poverty, although the ideal of apostolic poverty was evident in their lifestyle. They did, however, swear oaths of chastity.[20]

In the greater context of medieval religious movements the beguines take their place alongside the new monastic orders of the Augustinian Canons, Premonstratensians and Cistercians, and alongside the new mendicant orders of the Dominicans and Franciscans, as part of the popular reform movement triggered by the desire of Pope Gregory VII (reigned 1073–85) to restructure earthly society in accordance with what was understood to be a properly organised Christian world.[21] The Gregorian reform movement came to be interpreted as a call to emulate the example of Christ in the leading of a *vita apostolica*. In their espousal of apostolic poverty, there was a clear spiritual affinity between the beguines and the mendicant orders.

Unlike the monastic and mendicant orders, the beguines had no saintly founder. They first emerged as a number of loosely connected communities in the Low Countries, in particular in the diocese of Liège, in the late twelfth century. As the diocese of Liège belonged to the archdiocese of Cologne within the Holy Roman Empire, its bishops were often German and so it is unsurprising that the first beguine communities within the German-speaking world sprang up in the north-west of the kingdom of Germany.[22] In the thirteenth century, beguine communities were most numerous in towns from Osnabrück in the north, along the banks of the Rhine, to Basle in the south. However, there were also significant numbers of beguines scattered across towns in the northern and eastern German-speaking territories.

---

20 Cf. Devlin (1984: 189ff.).
21 As Pope, St Gregory (*c*. 1021–85) worked for the reform and moral revival of the Church. He issued decrees against simony (selling or purchasing of ecclesiastical offices) and nicolaitism (clerical marriage or concubinage) in 1074. In 1075 he forbade lay investiture (the right of lay rulers to grant church officials the symbols of their authority and to receive homage from them before their consecration). This latter measure aroused great controversy, especially in Germany, France and England.
22 Germany did not, of course, exist within the medieval context in the geographical and political shape that we are familiar with today. The German kingdom of the thirteenth century comprised a number of lordships that enjoyed considerable independence while sharing, to a variable extent, in common social, cultural and political traditions.

Poised between the monastic and the secular worlds, the beguinal way of life was in part characterised by its diversity. This is nowhere more evident than in the living arrangements of the beguines, who might be single, married or widowed (but who all took an oath of chastity). In the course of the thirteenth century four different patterns emerged. Some women who became beguines continued to live in their parental or their own homes, others set up house together, sometimes as an informal association and sometimes as a formally organised beguine convent. The numbers living in such a convent could vary from as few as two or three to as many as sixty or seventy women. Officially, the beguines were laywomen living in an established parish and thus in the spiritual care of the local clergy.[23] Where there was a particular concentration of beguines, of two to three hundred, they would form their own parishes, a walled-in 'town within a town'.[24] These 'beguinages' were a feature of beguinal life that was found almost exclusively in the Low Countries. Finally, some beguines adopted a life of wandering mendicancy, a pattern of life that attracted much censure in the course of the thirteenth century.

We have no documentary evidence of Mechthild's living arrangements in Magdeburg, but there is some circumstantial evidence in her writings that indicate she may have lived in a beguine convent. Thus, on one occasion Mechthild complains to God: 'In my community there is a religious person who causes me much distress because of her bad behaviour, for this person will not obey me in anything' (VI, 7 [p. 109]).[25] This remark further suggests that Mechthild had authority within her community, acting perhaps as the *magistra*.[26]

The beguines were one of the manifestations of a surge in female piety that extended from the late twelfth well into the mid-thirteenth century. Although a number of social and economic, as well as demographic factors have been suggested as causes for the exponential interest in the religious life among women,[27] fundamental to the

---

23 Cf. Devlin (1984: 184).

24 McDonnell (1954/69: 479).

25 Cf. also VI, 37, 63–64.

26 The majority of beguines who lived communally were under the jurisdiction of a *magistra*, much as a nun was subject to the authority of an abbess.

27 E.g. the effects of urbanisation on employment patterns and economic wealth, the depression of the independent status of aristocratic women through primogeniture; the longevity of women, the loss of men in battle and their absence on crusade, the numbers of men entering the priesthood. Cf. Shahar (1983: 53).

phenomenon of this widespread female religiosity was the explicit desire of many women to lead an evangelical life of poverty and chastity.[28] This religious impulse is exemplified in the life of Marie of Oignies (1176/77–1216), the prototype of the beguine. At fourteen, Marie was married to a man of her parents' choosing. However, Marie's early interest in the concept of voluntary personal poverty and her determination to lead a religious life shaped the course of her marriage. She distributed her wealth to the poor and persuaded her husband to take a vow of chastity with her. The couple went to Willambroux, outside Nivelles, where they devoted themselves to a leper colony. After a number of years, Marie, with the consent of her husband, moved to the Augustinian priory of St. Nicholas of Oignies sur Sambre where she lived as a lay sister. Here she led an ascetic, devotional life, supporting herself by spinning. Marie became a charismatic figure for the priory and in particular for the laywomen attached to it.

Our knowledge of Marie is conditioned by the laudatory life, *Vita Mariae Oigniacensis*, written by Marie's great admirer, the Augustinian Canon Jacques of Vitry (*c.* 1145–1240). Jacques extolled the beguinal way of life, drawing attention not only to the chastity, poverty, asceticism and manual labour practised by these women, but also to the mystical experiences of many of them, in particular as a result of their devotion to the Eucharist.[29] As a keen observer of the various spiritual currents at work in the contemporary Church, he saw in the beguines a model of lay piety that could be used to counter the Albigensian heresy that was rife in the south of France.[30]

Caesarius of Heisterbach (*c.* 1180–1240), a Cistercian monk and chronicler, commented about the beguines: 'they live together with lay people in a secular manner, they are superior in religious fervour

---

28 Cf. McDonnell (1954/69: 81ff.), Bolton (1976: 147f. and 1999).
29 On the importance of eucharistic devotion amongst women mystics of the thirteenth century see Bynum (1984 and 1992). Mechthild addresses her fellow beguines on the subject of eucharistic devotion in III, 15 [p. 61f.] and the nuns in Helfta on the same subject in VII, 21 [p. 127f.].
30 The Albigensians, who flourished in southern France in the twelfth and thirteenth centuries, were a branch of the Cathars, a heretical Christian sect. The Cathars professed a neo-Manichaean dualism, that is that there are two principles or divine beings, one good and the other evil and that the material world is evil. They held that Christ did not suffer or rise again because he was an angel with a phantom body. Cathar doctrines struck at the roots of orthodox Christianity and of the political institutions of Christendom. The authorities of the Church and State united to attack them.

to many in the cloister: they are spiritual among the worldly, they are continent among those that seek the pleasure of the senses, they lead the life of a hermit in the midst of crowds'.[31] His laudatory remarks testify to the high regard in which beguines were held by a number of prominent churchmen in the early decades of the thirteenth century. There is evidence in Mechthild's writings that she too was esteemed in some local circles. Thus, for example, she reports how a canon who had been appointed deacon of the cathedral in Magdeburg had turned to her for advice when he felt uncertain of how to conduct himself in his new position (VI, 2 [p. 107]).

Despite the approbation the beguines enjoyed from some quarters, they were nonetheless a vulnerable group in society because of their extra-regular status. In the course of the thirteenth century, the suspicion of heresy, which had dogged them from the outset, became increasingly acute, as witnessed in one of the reports prepared for the debate on the reform of the Church at the Second Council of Lyons in 1274. In the *Collectio de scandalis ecclesiae* ['Collection of Ecclesiastical Offences'] the Franciscan Gilbert of Tournai, reporting on the state of the Church in Northern France and Belgium, expresses alarm at the way beguines met 'in conventicles, in secret corners, in public squares' to read the Holy Scriptures in the vernacular and to interpret the 'mysteries of the scriptures' without proper guidance.[32] One of the other reports presented at the Council of Lyons by Bruno, the Bishop of Olomouc (in the present day Czech Republic), complains that women leading a beguinal way of life were using their liberty both to escape the bonds of marriage and the obedience required of them by their parish priests. The threat of heresy is palpable in Mechthild's writings: 'I was warned about this book and people told me that if it were not protected, it would be burnt' (II, 26 [p. 47]) and 'Now I am afraid of God, if I keep quiet and yet I am afraid of ignorant people if I write' (III, 1 [p. 52]).

Although Mechthild frequently expresses her sense of vulnerability as an uneducated woman writing at the command of God,[33] it is clear from the prefaces to the *FL* and from the prologue to the *Ld* that she had the support of the Dominicans. The approbation of the Order that gave such central importance to study must have provided

---

[31] Translated from the Latin as quoted in McDonnell (1954/69: 224f.).

[32] Translated from the German translation as quoted in Grundmann (1935/77: 336f.).

[33] E.g. II, 26 (p. 47); III, 1 (p. 56); IV, 2 (p. 73).

Mechthild with some protection from her critics. The German preface to the *FL* tells us that 'a brother of this same Order compiled this book and copied it'. In the *Ld* this brother is identified as 'Brother Heinrich, said to be from Halle, a lector from Ruppin'.[34] The extent to which Heinrich of Halle might have been involved in the shaping of Mechthild's book has been a subject of some controversy. According to Neumann, whose findings underlie most of the subsequent scholarship on this issue,[35] Heinrich edited the first six books of the *FL*. He considers Heinrich to have been a careful and respectful editor who altered little of Mechthild's wording, his principal contribution being the division of the material into books and possibly the provision of titles for some of the chapters.[36]

Mechthild reciprocates the respect of the Dominicans through eulogising in her writings the Order and their founding father in particular. Thus, she declares she loves Dominic above all other saints (IV, 20 [p. 77]) and she has visions in which she sees how the Dominicans will be greatly rewarded and honoured in Heaven for their efforts on earth (III, 1 [p. 53]). Despite the vision of this heavenly reward, Mechthild is nonetheless critical of the Dominicans; she feels the Order has lost some of its initial drive and inspiration and she takes the Friars to task for their neglect of pastoral duties: 'O you preachers, how reluctantly you now set your tongue to work and how unwillingly you bend your ear to the sinner's mouth' (III, 1 [p. 54]).[37] These chiding remarks of Mechthild have a polemic edge, for throughout the thirteenth century the matter of priestly office and the administering of the sacraments proved to be a source of considerable tension between the secular clergy and the Dominicans. Papal rulings on this matter varied widely. In a letter dated 14 February 1221 to the prelates of the Christian world, Honorius III emphasises how the Dominicans are not only called to preach, but also to hear confessions, but, in his bull *Etsi animarum* of 21 November 1254, Innocent IV withdrew the privileges of the mendicant order with

---

[34] *Ld*: 516, 23–5.

[35] Cf. Ruh (1993: 249ff.) and Tobin (1995a: 1ff.)

[36] Neumann (1954/64: 176). Peters (1988) gives a radical re-assessment of biographical information concerning Heinrich in the *FL* and the *Ld* and comes to the conclusion that any conjecture about Heinrich's association with Mechthild rests on an 'uncertain historical basis' (p. 117). Peters interprets the role of Heinrich merely in terms of his function within the conventions of the 'call to write' topos, that is that Heinrich was the confessor figure to whom the holy woman experiencing visions would turn to for advice and guidance.

[37] See also VI, 1, 10–12.

regard to preaching, the hearing of confession and burial rites, while Martin IV in his bull of 13 December 1281, *Ad fructus uberes*, freed the Order of Preachers from episcopal control, allowing the Friars Preachers to work in the parishes without restriction. A synod held in Magdeburg by Archbishop Rupert in 1261 gives a local context for the controversial nature of Mechthild's remarks.[38] This synod reminded beguines that they must obey their parish priests as other parishioners did, that is they should not evade the control and supervision of the clergy by preferring Dominicans as their confessors and spiritual advisers. Failure to follow the demands of the synod would result in excommunication.

Further evidence of the esteem in which Mechthild held the Preaching Order and her readiness to take their part in conflicts with the secular clergy is evident in her apocalyptic vision in Book IV. She opens the account of this vision by remarking: 'The Order of Preachers had come under heavy fire from false masters, and from many greedy sinners too' (IV, 27 [p. 79]). This is an allusion to the bitter attack of William of St Amour and other professors in Paris on the mendicant orders in the 1250s.[39] In the course of her apocalyptic vision Mechthild prophesies the advent of an order that will be modelled on the Order of Preachers, but whose members 'shall be wiser and more powerful and have fewer earthly needs and be more fired with the Holy Spirit' (IV, 27 [p. 80]) and, polemically, she reports: 'Wherever they go, the right to preach, hear confession, sing and read the Mass is not denied them' (IV, 27 [p. 82]).

Life as a nun

What prompted Mechthild to enter the convent at Helfta during the last years of her life is unclear. Certainly, Mechthild talks increasingly in the *FL* of the hostile reception accorded to herself and her writings[40] and the author of the prologue to the *Ld* comments: 'Finally, in her old age, after many troubles, she entered the cloistered life at Helfta' (*Ld*: 436, 30–1). Her withdrawal from secular life may also have been in response to the wave of negative opinion on the beguinal way of life reflected in the reports of Gilbert of Tournai and Bruno, Bishop of Olomouc, at the Council of Lyons in 1274.

---

38 Cf. Grundmann (1935/77: 33, n. 24).
39 Schmidt (1995: 381f., n. 174) draws attention to a marginal note in Ms B of the *Ld* which identifies the 'false masters': 'Gulielmi a Sancto Amore etc. in Universitate Parisiensi'.
40 E.g. VI, 31 (p. 115); VI, 36 (p. 116f.); VI, 38 (p. 117).

Perhaps, too, her health was already failing, moving her to seek the greater security of the convent, for in the penultimate passage of Book VII Mechthild thanks God for the assistance given her by her fellow nuns: 'Lord, I thank you that, since you have taken my eyesight from me, you now serve me with the eyes of others. Lord, I thank you that, since you have taken the strength of my hands, you now serve me with the hands of others' (VII, 64 [p. 138]).

The convent of St Mary at Helfta was founded in 1229 by Elisabeth of Schwarzburg and her husband, Burchard, Count of Mansfeld. The first nuns at Helfta were Benedictines who, however, followed the customs of the Cistercian Order without being affiliated with it.[41] When Mechthild went to Helfta in *c.* 1270 it was a prestigious establishment renowned for its artistic culture and its literary production. During the abbacy of Gertrude of Hackeborn (1232–91), particular attention was paid to the education of the nuns:

> She [Gertrude] would read sacred scripture very eagerly and with great delight whenever she could, requiring her subjects to love sacred readings and often recite them from memory. Hence, she bought all the good books she could for her church or made her sisters transcribe them. She eagerly promoted the girls to learn the liberal arts, saying that if the pursuit of knowledge were lost they would no longer understand sacred scripture and the religious life would also perish.[42]

To judge from a passage addressed to her fellow nuns, this pronounced emphasis on learning may well have been daunting for Mechthild who had earlier recorded that she knew no Latin and was uneducated:[43] 'You want teaching from me and yet I am myself uneducated. That which you constantly thirst for you can find a thousand times in your books' (VII, 21 [p. 127]). Despite this assertion of inadequacy, Mechthild goes on in this passage to give instruction based on her experiential knowledge of God, further highlighting the contrast which she establishes polemically throughout her work between knowledge of God derived from book learning and direct

---

41 In 1228 the General Chapter of the Cistercian Order, in an attempt to stabilise their commitment to the *cura monialium* ('spiritual care of cloistered women'), had forbidden the foundation of any further communities of nuns and the additional spiritual supervision of communities already in existence.

42 The passage is taken from Gertrude the Great's *Legatus divinae pietatis*, quoted from McGinn (1998: 446, n. 267).

43 Cf. II, 3, 48 and II, 26 (p. 48).

knowledge of God received through grace. However, in Helfta Mechthild was among kindred spirits. Two younger contemporaries, Mechthild of Hackeborn (1241– *c*. 1298) and Gertrude the Great (1256– *c*. 1301), were visionary charismatics. By the end of the thirteenth century, the books recording the revelations and visions accorded to Mechthild and Gertrude, the *Liber specialis gratiae* ['The Book of Special Grace'] and *Legatus divinae pietatis* ['The Herald of Divine Love'], together with Mechthild of Magdeburg's *FL*, represented 'the largest single body of women's mystical writing of the period'.[44]

The Flowing Light of the Godhead

Private revelations

The Dominican author of the prologue to the *Ld* describes Mechthild's text as 'revelations and visions'.[45] Mechthild's writings may be described, at least in part, as 'private revelations', that is they are presented as a record of what God has revealed to her. The term 'private revelations' is used in contradistinction to 'public revelation'. Public revelation refers to what is recorded in the Bible as God's self-revelation to mankind through the Prophets and Apostles. The 'deposit of faith' revealed to man was complete with the incarnation of God in Christ. It is the task of the ordained successors of the Apostles, that is, the bishops and, through their license, priests, both to continue to transmit Christian revelation and to comprehend the 'deposit of faith' in their preaching. However, since the death of the last Apostle, some individuals have been graced with private revelations which are considered by the Catholic Church to be 'a normal manifestation of the presence of the Spirit of Christ in the Mystical Body and of His continued guidance of the Church. Without bringing anything new to the Catholic Faith, they draw attention to what in the faith is likely to meet the particular needs of the times.'[46]

Like public revelation, private revelations carry with them the mandate to proclaim the knowledge received from God. In his account of the charisms that were granted for the good of all to some individuals who held no office in the nascent Church, Paul mentions

---

44 Bynum (1982: 174).

45 '[R]evelationes et visiones' (*Ld*: 473, 3).

46 De Letter (1967: 447).

the gift of prophecy, or speaking in the name of God.[47] Thus, alongside the authorised preaching of the Church, there was another tradition of preaching that derived its authority directly from God. This
was a tradition open to women who were otherwise excluded from
positions of authority in the patriarchal Church. The invocation of
the authority derived from private revelations, expressed through the
divine 'call to write' topos, became a commonplace in the visionary
writings of women of the twelfth, thirteenth and fourteenth centuries.[48]

The issue of the authorship, and hence the authority, of the *FL* is
one of the central concerns of Mechthild's text. She is at pains to de-
lineate clearly the parameters within which she is writing. Thus, she
portrays herself as merely fulfilling the demands of the 'call to write'
topos imposed upon her: ' "Ah Lord, now I am distressed because of
Your honour, if You do not comfort me now, then You have misled
me, for You ordered me to write it Yourself" ' (II, 26 [p. 47]).
Mechthild records for her readers the reassurance God gives her that
ultimately He is the author of her book:

> 'This book is threefold and signifies me alone. This parch-
> ment, which encloses it, signifies my pure, white and just
> humanity that suffered death for your sake. The words
> signify my wondrous Godhead; they flow hour by hour into
> your soul out of my divine mouth. The tone of the words
> signifies my living spirit and through this the full truth is
> realised.'   (II, 26 [p. 47f.])

This divine reassurance is further strengthened by Mechthild's
account of how she confided in her confessor, who confirmed the
authenticity of Mechthild's visions and revelations and ordered her
to write down what she had been graced with. Thus, Mechthild presents her authorship of the *FL* as an act of religious obedience:[49]

> Then he instructed me to do what often gives me cause me to
> weep for shame, for I am acutely aware of my own unworthi-
> ness, that is he ordered a pitiful woman to write this book out

---

[47]   1 Corinthians 12: 7–11 and 28–30; Romans 12: 6–8; Ephesians 4: 11–13.

[48]   Voaden (1995: 57) identifies three ways in which the 'call to write' topos could be
realised: (i) some divine figure explicitly commands the visionary to write, (ii) the
visionary represents her writing as inspired directly by God, (iii) the visionary's
completed writing is given the divine imprimatur.

[49]   Heimbach (1989: 151). Religious obedience is one of Mechthild's central
concerns in the *FL* and is the most frequently cited failing of those leading the life
of the religious, cf. V, 5 (p. 88f.); V, 8 (p. 90); V, 16 (p. 92).

of the heart and mouth of God. Thus this book has come lovingly from God and is not drawn from human senses.

(IV, 2 [p. 73])

Mechthild repeatedly expresses an acute awareness of her own vulnerability as an uneducated woman in communicating what God has revealed to her.[50] Her temerity is justified, however, through the representation of herself within that paradigm, familiar from hagiography, of *sancta simplicitas* ['holy simplicity']; that is, where the holy person's lack of formal education and their reliance on the Holy Spirit are taken as evidence of the authenticity of their experiences and consequently become a weapon with which to disarm potential opponents. Thus God tells Mechthild:

> One finds many a wise master versed in scripture, who is, however, a fool in my eyes. And I'll tell you something else: With regard to them, it is a great honour to me and strengthens holy Christianity considerably that the untutored mouth, inspired by the Holy Spirit, instructs the learned tongue.   (II, 26 [p. 48])[51]

Literary classification

Mechthild's writings, as they are encompassed in the Einsiedeln manuscript, comprise two prefaces, one in Latin and one in Middle High German, and 267 chapters that are ordered into seven books. The volume of the chapters varies considerably, some are only a few lines in length, others run to several pages. Some of the chapters cluster together thematically and structurally, but the majority of them are free standing. The heterogeneous and discrete nature of the individual chapters is, however, offset by Mechthild's strong sense of the unity of her writings. In a number of key passages where she comments on the co-authorship of her work by God and herself, she invariably and programmatically refers to her writings as a 'book'.[52] Nonetheless, the idiosyncratic and diverse nature of Mechthild's writings elude categorisation as an integral literary work, encompassing and fusing as they do visions, auditions, dialogues, prayers, hymns, lyrical love poems, letters, allegories, parables and narratives, as well as features derived from the hagiographical life, the

---

[50] E.g. II, 26 (p. 47f.); III, 1 (p. 52); V, 12 (p. 91); VII, 8 (p. 126); VII, 36 (p. 131).
[51] This passage has its scriptural underpinning in 1 Corinthians 1: 27–28. Cf. Matthew 11: 26 and Luke 10: 21.
[52] E.g. II, 26 (p. 47); III, 20 (p. 63); IV, 2 (p. 70); V, 12 (p. 91); V, 34 (p. 101).

disputation, the treatise, and magic spells. As the narrator, Mechthild casts herself in the role of visionary, lover, mystic, prophet, teacher, critic, counsellor and intercessor. There are no generic models for Mechthild's writings as an integral work. However, in a broad sense Mechthild's writings may be placed within that tradition of religious individuality initiated by St Augustine (354–430) in his *Confessions*. Like the *Confessions*, the *FL* is an intimate dialogue with God, narrated essentially in the first person. It was Augustine's intention that his dialogue be 'overheard' and reflected on by his fellow Christians and so too is Mechthild's expression of the greatness of God's love for her not an exclusive, private message, but an exemplary message for all. Like Augustine's work, the *FL* is confessional in its devotional outpourings of both penitence and thanksgiving.[53]

Although the *FL* defies classification in terms of genre, in terms of mystical discourse the relevant passages in the text present a clear profile. Mechthild's mystical writings may be grouped under the heading of affective mysticism, for it is essentially through love that Mechthild seeks and experiences union with the Godhead.[54] Furthermore, the lyrical quality of Mechthild's language may be readily described as cataphatic or affirmative in nature, that is, it is characterised by a rich and creative use of metaphor and analogy. The technical term 'cataphatic', drawn from the vocabulary of late Platonist Christian theology, contrasts with apophatic or negative discourse where all ideas and images of God are rejected as an inadequate description of what God is.[55] Cataphatic and apophatic discourse are complementary rather than mutually exclusive, for both types of discourse struggle to convey the ineffability of the Godhead, ultimately recognising 'that all speech about God must end in silence'.[56] Thus, despite all the wealth of the imagery Mechthild employs to convey her apprehension and awareness of God, she nonetheless on a number of occasions expresses her frustration at the inadequacy of what she has communicated, drawing attention both to her own limitations and the limitations of language: 'The bliss, the glory, the

---

[53] Cf. Haas (1972: 111) and Ruh (1993: 256). For a discussion of both similarities and dissimilarities in the form and intention of Augustine's *Confessions* and the *FL*, see Hollywood (1995: 57ff.).

[54] By contrast, speculative mysticism makes greater use of the intellect and reason.

[55] Mechthild does, occasionally, also make use of apophatic language, cf. I, 35 [p. 33].

[56] McGinn (1998: 230).

brightness, the loving embrace, the truth – this is so overwhelming that I fell silent, unable to speak anymore about what I know' (VI, 41 [p. 117]).[57]

Selection of chapters for translation

The upsurge of interest in women's writing in the wake of feminist criticism and gender studies has led to a proliferation of anthologies in English of selected texts by medieval women. Passages from the *FL* have been regularly included.[58] However, the constraints of an anthology dictate, of course, that only a limited selection of Mechthild's writings has been included, typically the lyrical passages focused on mystical union. An anthology solely of Mechthild's writings was compiled by Margot Schmidt for inclusion in a series entitled 'Texte zum Nachdenken' ['Texts for Reflection'].[59] Schmidt's method of selection was to extract passages from their context in the individual chapters and group them together under such headings as 'The Call to Write', 'What is the Soul?', 'Paths to God', 'Angels and Devils'. By arranging the material in this way, Schmidt has facilitated our insight into the contours of the theological world which Mechthild inhabits and brought to the fore the devotional aspect of Mechthild's writings, but the integrity of the passages as pieces of creative writing has been violated.

In making my selection of passages from the *FL* I have chosen to respect the integrity of the individual chapters.[60] I have also accepted the premise that the material is, broadly speaking, in chronological order and so have left the chapters in the order in which they occur in Neumann's critical edition, retaining the division of the material into seven books.[61] Mechthild herself seems to identify three distinct periods in the course of her life. She reports God saying to her: 'Your childhood was a companion to my Holy Spirit, your youth was a bride to my Humanity, your old age is now a wife to my Godhead' (VII, 3 [p. 124]) and she reflects on how the manner in which God

---

57 Cf. V, 12 [p. 91].
58 Cf. Wilson (1984), Petroff (1986), Bowie (1989), and Larrington (1995).
59 Schmidt (1988).
60 The translated passages in this book constitute approximately forty-five per cent of the entire text.
61 Neumann (1954/64) identifies three distinct stages in the evolution of the *FL*: Books I–V, Book VI, Book VII. In his opinion Books I–V constitute an early unit and within this he recognises a further structural unity in Books I–IV. Cf. Kemper (1979).

has bestowed grace upon her has changed with the passage of time: 'God has given this gift, which is written in this book, in three ways to me. First of all with great tenderness, then most intimately, now with much pain' (VI, 20, 4–6). This sense of chronology is enhanced by a shift in the dominant tone of the constituent books. The lyrical, exclamatory and spontaneous quality of the early books gives way to more reflection, a certain distance, a greater use of allegory and a greater involvement in mundane matters as the work progresses. Furthermore, in the course of Mechthild's writings there is a growing sense of Mechthild's self-assurance and authority, as evidenced in her comments on the proper conduct of the religious life.[62] In my choice of passages I have sought to reflect these changes in tone and style.

The structure of my anthology is intended to offer the reader pathways through a text that is, on first acquaintance, confusing in its heterogeneity and diversity. Thus, my selection of chapters was further determined by the dominance and prevalence of certain themes, for example, the union of the Soul with God, the self-projection of Mechthild as 'author' and 'narrator', Mechthild's relationship with her contemporaries (fellow beguines and nuns, Dominicans, the secular clergy), her visionary visitations to Heaven, Paradise, Purgatory and Hell. The occurrence of these salient themes is identified in the brief introductions I have provided for each of the seven books. The chapters chosen are also intended to reflect both the rich diversity of register and discourse woven into the texture of Mechthild's writings in her use of, for example, allegorical exegesis, disputational dialogue, hymnic praise, the love lyric, the naïve narrative of the fairy story, anaphoric rhetorical address, everyday idiomatic expressions and aphorisms.[63]

Translation of the selected chapters
My translation of Mechthild's writings is informed throughout by the apparatus to Neumann's edition and the accompanying volume of textual notes and studies, as well as the notes appended to Schmidt's and Tobin's translations. On occasion I make specific reference to these valuable sources of information in my own footnotes, but generally I have chosen not to burden the newcomer to the text with editorial detail.

---

[62] Cf. Poor (1994: 101) and Hollywood (1995: 65).
[63] Cf. Mohr (1963) and Hellgardt (1996).

One of the fascinating aspects of Mechthild's writings is the protean quality of the medium in which she writes. In his edition of the *FL* Morel divided Mechthild's text sharply into prose and verse, making it appear as if it were written in the tradition of prosimetrum, that is, where there is, within one text, a switch from prose to verse and back again.[64] However, Mechthild's style is much more fluid than this would suggest. Peter Dronke talks of the 'lyrical continuum' of the *FL* that 'extends from the rhythmic prose, filled with parallelism and homoioteleuta, to more sustained rhymed passages, to fully poetic forms'.[65] Mechthild uses a variety of rhyme schemes such as impure rhyme, identical rhyme and cases where a rhyme occurs in an accented syllable of one word and in an unaccented syllable of another word. However, the most characteristic feature of Mechthild's rhyming patterns is her use of what is known in Mechthild scholarship as 'colon rhyme',[66] that is, she uses assonance rhyme to link together segments of sentences in her prose.[67] The occurrence of colon rhyme in the *FL* is variable, but there is a distinct tendency towards increased use of it as a chapter comes to a close, which sometimes transmutes into verse. In his edition of the *FL* Neumann employed expanded spacing to highlight the presence of colon rhyme. The following passage may serve to illustrate the occurrence of this phenomenon and Neumann's representation of it:[68]

---

64 As, for example, in Boethius' *De consolatione Philosophiae* ['On the Consolation of Philosophy'].

65 Dronke (1994: 217). Homoioteleuton is a rhetorical figure that first occurs in Aristotle's writings on rhetoric. It is the recurrence of word endings in inflected languages that sound the same (e.g. 'mone<u>bant</u>, fere<u>bant</u> and iude<u>bant</u>') in successive words, or in successive parts of a sentence in successive shorter sentences. It is often used to highlight parallelism and antithesis. It may be regarded as a precursor of rhyme.

66 Neumann (1990: XXII). Colon is used here in the sense of a syntactic or rhetorical phrase, usually marked off by punctuation, which combines with comparable phrases to articulate the meaning of a sentence (cf. the punctuation marks colon [:] and semi-colon [;]).

67 Tobin (1998: 21) notes: 'More frequent than rhyme as it is normally understood – as the correspondence of vowel and consonant sounds at the end of a word (can–man; token–broken) – are occurrences of assonance or vowel rhyme, where only the vowels correspond (can–fat; token–over).'

68 Some occurrences of this colon rhyme were lost in the fourteenth-century transposition of Mechthild's Low German into High German, cf. Neumann (1990: XXII).

'Herre, nu bin ich ein nakent sele und du in dir selben ein wolgezieret g o t . Únser zweiger gemeinschaft ist das ewige lip ane t o t .' So geschihet da ein selig s t i l l i nach ir beider w i l l e n . Er gibet sich ir und si git sich i m e . Was ir nu g e s c h e h e , das weis s i , und des getroeste ich m i c h . nu dis mag nit lange s t a n ; wa zwoei geliebe verholen zesamen koment, si muessent dike ungescheiden von einander g a n .

Lieber gottes frúnt, disen minneweg han ich dir g e s c h r i b e n , got muesse in an din herze g e b e n ! Amen.

(I, 44, 88–95)

'Lord, now I am a naked soul and you in yourself a richly adorned God. Our communion together is eternal life without death.' Then a blessed stillness follows that they both desire. He gives Himself to her and she herself to Him. What may happen to her now, she knows, and I comfort myself with that. Now this cannot last long; where two lovers come together secretly, they must often leave one another without separating.

Dear friend of God, I have written down this path of love for you, may God favour your heart with it! Amen.

(I, 44 [p. 36])

I have not attempted to render this complex texture of rhyme assonance into English and so it is, unfortunately, completely absent in my translation. In the layout of the text, I have followed Neumann rather than Schmidt and Tobin. Thus, my prose translation is presented as prose, except where the writings are unequivocally in verse form in Neumann's edition. Schmidt and Tobin, by contrast, make greater use of Morel's model, drawing a sharper distinction between what might be classified on the one hand as prose and on the other as verse.[69]

The act of transposing a text from one language into another raises a number of challenging issues about which the translator must make a decision. I have attempted to produce a faithful translation which will allow the reader, should he or she so wish, to find themselves quickly in the Middle High German text, but at the same time

---

[69] Schmidt manages in many instances to find equivalent rhyme schemes in the verse in her modern German. Although he does not cast his English into rhyme, Tobin nonetheless visually presents corresponding passages as verse in the layout on the page.

I have striven to ensure that the translated text is fully comprehensible within itself. English has a far richer vocabulary than Middle High German and this allows considerable scope for a translation that is nuanced in its interpretation. However, wherever an item of vocabulary recurs frequently in similar contexts, I have sought to be consistent in my translation of this word so that the reader may more readily identify those central ideas, concerns and emotions that preoccupy Mechthild.

Another distinctive feature of Mechthild's writing is the 'spoken' quality of her style.[70] Her narrative is frequently progressed by an adverbial series of 'do . . . do . . . do . . .' [then . . . then . . . then . . .]. Although this can appear clumsy to the silent reader of the written word, I have chosen not to smooth this over, preferring instead to let the reader feel the staccato effect of such passages of narrative. This 'spoken' quality of Mechthild's language can also, on occasion, lead to rather unwieldy sentence construction. Here too, I have decided not to interfere with the structure of such sentences. A further aspect of this 'spoken' nature of Mechthild's writings is her emphatic use of dramatic dialogue.[71] The canvas of the *FL* encompasses the Christian universe in time and space and so Mechthild engages with figures drawn from the celestial and infernal regions, from biblical history as well as from her circle of contemporaries. Furthermore, Mechthild has personifications such as the Soul, the Body, Love, Constancy and Pain enter into dialogue with her and with each other. To enhance the reader's awareness of this dialogic feature I have used capital letters to identify personifications that assume a speaking presence in the text. In similar vein, I have also consistently used capitals for pronouns referring to the persons of the Trinity, that the reader may be constantly reminded of the divine nature of Mechthild's interlocutors.

In perhaps the most well-known chapter of the *FL*, I, 44, Mechthild concludes, as quoted above, with an address to her readers: 'Dear friend of God, I have written down this path of love for you, may God favour your heart with it' (I, 44 [p. 36]). She has sought to translate through mystical imagery, personification and allegory her experience of the path of the individual soul to ecstatic union with God. In an analogous sense, the translator of an imaginative foreign text is obliged to try and retrace the path of the author

---

[70] Cf. Grubmüller (1992).
[71] Cf. Grubmüller (1992), Haug (1984), Largier (1987), and Tillmann (1933).

from the text back to the state of mind and feeling which produced it in the first place and then to produce, as it were, a parallel path. It is my hope that the translations that follow will provide such a parallel path, affording the English speaker with no knowledge of German some insight into the quality and nature of Mechthild's writings.

Selections from
The Flowing Light of the Godhead

Prologue[1]

This book should be received with joy, for the words are spoken by God Himself

This book I now send as a messenger to all religious people, worthy and unworthy alike, for if the pillars collapse then the building cannot remain standing, and it reveals me alone and tells of the mystery of my intimacy in praise.[2] All those who would understand this book should read it nine times.

This book is called a flowing light of the Godhead

'Ah, Lord God, who has made this book?' 'I have made it out of weakness, for I cannot contain my gift.' 'Ah Lord, what should this book be called in honour of You alone?' 'It shall be called a light flowing from my Godhead into all those hearts that live free of falsehood.'

---

[1] There is a short prologue to the seven books of the *FL* as they have been edited from Ms E, the first section of which, at least, would appear to have been a later addition to the work and not from Mechthild's hand (Neumann 1954/64: 182f.). Certainly, this prologue does not appear in the list of contents for Book I. With the exception of the final sentence, thought to have been added in the mid-fourteenth century, the first part of the Prologue is a welding together of some key statements about the nature and function of Mechthild's 'book' made by the persona of God (V, 34 [p. 101]; II, 26 [p. 47]) in the course of the *FL*.

[2] The interpretation of this short prologue to the *FL* has aroused controversy in Mechthild scholarship (for a summary of conflicting opinions see Andersen 2000: 123). Is the speaker of this passage to be identified as God or Mechthild? The controversy centres on the interpretation of the phrase 'mine heimlichkeit'. Through an analysis of the 17 occurrences of this term, Heimbach-Steins (1995) demonstrates Mechthild's use of the word to refer both to God's mystery in the sense of His self-revelation and to Mechthild's intimacy with God through her mystical encounters with Him. Heimbach-Steins argues convincingly for embracing the inherent ambiguity of the phrase as it occurs in the Prologue and thus for hearing God's voice in Mechthild's (1995: 86). I too have argued for the 'double-voicing' of the Prologue (2000: 123). My difficulty in translating this passage has been to convey this ambiguity adequately in English. The two voices of God and Mechthild are separated out in the second part of the Prologue where they engage in a dialogue about the origin of the book.

Book I

Book I is the most lyrical of the seven. It is characterised by a sense of the immediacy, intimacy and exclusiveness of the loving Soul's relationship with God. Love is identified as the primal force in the Christian universe. For Mechthild, Love is both a personified figure in her metaphysical drama and the defining attribute of God. Attention is drawn to the conflict that exists between the Body and the Soul (I, 2; I, 5; I, 44), a conflict that is to persist throughout Mechthild's writings, although there is eventually a harmonious reconciliation between the two at the very end of the book (VII, 65).

In this book, the origin, history and the nature of the Soul are described and placed within the context of salvation history (I, 22; I, 44). However, it is the exemplary account of the Soul's path to and experience of union with God that has primacy (I, 2; I, 4; I, 44). In her expression of the quality of the love shared by the Soul and God, Mechthild draws creatively on a stock of mystical imagery culled pre-eminently from biblical and neo-platonic sources, but also from the court, the tavern, and the context of everyday life. Elemental images of fire, water and light, dynamic images of flowing, sinking and soaring, images of courtship and sexual union, of dancing and drinking abound and are to resonate throughout the entire text (I, 4; I, 5; I, 17–21; I, 23–24; I, 44).

Dialogue is the key structural feature of this Book, dialogue between the Soul and Love (I, 1), between the Soul and the Body (I, 2; I, 5; I, 44), between God and the loving Soul (I, 17–21; 23–24), Christ and the loving Soul (I, 44), the Virgin Mary and the loving Soul (I, 22), between Mechthild and those loving souls who seek instruction on the path to union with God (I, 2; I, 35; I, 44).

I, 1. How Love and the Queen spoke together
The Soul came to Love and greeted her with great respect and said: 'May God greet you, Lady Love.' 'May God reward you, Majesty.' 'Lady Love, you are truly perfect.' 'Majesty, that is why I am above all things.' 'Lady Love, you struggled for many years before you brought the exalted Trinity to pour itself into Mary's humble virginity.' 'Majesty, that is to your honour and greater good.' 'Lady Love, now you have come to me and stripped me of everything that I

ever acquired on Earth.' 'Majesty, you have made a blessed exchange.' 'Lady Love, you have robbed me of my childhood.' 'Majesty, in return I have given you heavenly freedom.' 'Lady Love, you have robbed me of all my youth.' 'Majesty, in return I have given you many holy virtues.' 'Lady Love, you have stripped me of property, friends and family.' 'Ah, Majesty, this is a complaint unworthy of you.' 'Lady Love, you have taken the world, worldly honour and all worldly wealth from me.' 'Majesty, together with the Holy Spirit, I can recompense you in just one hour for all your earthly desires.' 'Lady Love, you have put me under such pressure that my body is overcome by a strange weakness.' 'Majesty, in return I have gifted you with much sublime insight.' 'Lady Love, you have consumed my flesh and my blood.' 'Majesty, in this way you have been purified and drawn into God.' 'Lady Love, you are a thief, but you shall make amends to me.' 'Majesty, then just take me myself.' 'Lady Love, now you have repaid me a hundred-fold on Earth.' 'Majesty, you still have God and all His kingdom to ask for.'

I, 2. Of three Persons and of three gifts

The true greeting of God, which issues forth from the heavenly flood out of the fountain of the flowing Trinity, has such mighty force that it deprives the Body of all its strength and reveals the Soul to herself so that she sees herself in the likeness of the saints and is then bathed in divine radiance.[3] Then the Soul departs from the Body with all her power, wisdom, love and desire, leaving only the smallest part of her living presence with the Body as in a sweet sleep. Then she sees a whole God in Three Persons and apprehends the Three Persons in a God undivided. Then He greets her in the language of the court, which is not heard in this kitchen, and dresses her in clothes that are fitting for the palace and puts Himself at her disposal. Then whatever she may wish for will be granted her and all her questions will be answered. What she is not told about is the prime cause of the Three Persons.[4] Then He draws her further to a secret place. There she must

---

[3]   Like Frank Tobin in his translation, I consistently identify the persona of the Soul as a feminine entity. Mechthild draws on the imagery of the Song of Songs in her presentation of the Soul as the bride of Christ and the Soul is regularly addressed as 'Lady'. Furthermore, although Mechthild refers to the Soul generically, within the context of her writings it is ultimately the experiences of her own soul that she is describing and it thus seems appropriate to give the Soul of the *FL* a feminine identity.

[4]   Neumann (1993: 5, n. I, 2, 13) draws attention to the puzzling phrase 'the prime

neither intercede nor plead for another, for neither the Body, nor the peasant at the plough, nor the knight at the tournament, nor His lovely mother Mary knows anything of the delight He seeks with her; the Soul may have nothing to do with them there. Thus they soar further to a wondrous place, of which I neither can nor will speak. It is too difficult, I dare not, for I am a very sinful person. To carry on: when the endless God brings the boundless Soul into the heights, she then loses sight of the Earth in the wonder of it all and cannot think that she was ever there. When the delight is at its very height that is when you have to leave it. Thus, God in full bloom says:[5] 'Young lady, you have to go back down.' Then she is shocked and weeps at her banishment. Then she says: ' Lord, You have now transported me so far that, within my body, I shall only be able to praise You as I should through suffering the pain of desolation and fighting against my body.' Then He says: 'O, you dear dove, your voice is the music of strings to my ears, your words are spices in my mouth, your desires are the bounty of my gift.' Then she says: 'Dear Lord, it must be as the Master of the house wishes.' Then she sighs so deeply that the Body stirs. Then the Body says: 'Well, Lady, now where have you been? You come back so full of love, beautiful and strong, free and sharp-witted. Your going off robbed me of my sense of taste and smell, of my colour and all my strength.' Then she says: 'Shut up, murderer, stop your moaning! I'll always be on my guard against you. It's of little concern to us that my enemy may be wounded, I'm glad about it.'

This is a greeting that has many channels; it constantly presses out of the flowing God into the poor, parched Soul with new insight and new revelation and with particular enjoyment of the new presence. O, sweet God, burning within and in full bloom without, since you have granted this to the lowest, I now want to experience the life you have given to your greatest, for this I would suffer all the more. No one can or may receive this greeting unless they have been outside of themselves and have become nothing. I want to die alive in this greeting;

cause of the Three Persons', suggesting that something has been lost from this sentence at an early stage of the transmission of the text. The passage remains equally obscure in the *Ld*.

5   The Middle High German word 'bluejend' ['blooming'] is one of the adjectives Mechthild characteristically uses to describe the fullness of God. Cf. III, 1 (p. 53); III, 15 (p. 61). This descriptive image has a long history as an epithet of God. Lüers (1926/1966: 136ff.) traces it back to the writings of Dionysius, the Pseudo-Areopagite (*c.* 500).

the blindly devout, that is those who love but have no insight, will never be able to ruin this for me.

I, 4. Of the Soul's journey to court, in the course of which God reveals Himself

Whenever the poor Soul comes to court, she is discerning and refined. Then she looks joyfully on her God. Ah, how lovingly she is received there! She then falls silent and longs intensely for His praise. Then He, with great desire, shows her His divine heart. It is like red gold burning in a great coal-fire. Then He puts her into His glowing heart. When the great Lord and the little maid thus embrace and are mingled as water and wine, then she becomes nothing and is enraptured. When she can cope no longer, then He is lovesick for her, as He always was, for He neither waxes nor wanes. Then she says: 'Lord, You are my loved one, my desire, my flowing fountain, my sun and I am Your mirror.'[6] This is a journey to court by the loving Soul that cannot exist without God.

I, 5. Of the torment and of the praise of the Soul

My body is in prolonged torment, my soul is in elated bliss, for she has both seen and embraced her Lover fully. He is the cause of her torment, poor wretch. Whenever He draws her up to Him, then she flows; she cannot stop until He has brought her into Himself. Then she would like to speak but cannot; through this sublime union she is completely caught up in the wonders of the Trinity. Then He withdraws a little so that she might feel desire. Then she longs for His praise that she cannot find just when she wants it. She even wishes that He might send her to Hell, so that He would be praised beyond measure by all creatures. Then she looks at Him and says to Him: 'Lord, give me Your blessing.' Then He looks at her and draws her to Him again and the greeting He gives her is beyond what the Body can express. Then the Body says to the Soul: 'Where have you been? I can't take any more.' Then the Soul says: 'Shut up, you're a fool. I want to be with my love even if that were to mean the end of you. I am His delight, He is my torment.' This is her torment; may she never recover from it! May you be overcome by this torment and may you never escape it.

---

6 On the history of the imagery of mirrors in mystical writing, see Schmidt (1995: 349, n. 19).

I, 17. The Soul praises God in five ways
O You outpouring God in Your giving, O You flowing God in Your love, O You burning God in Your desire, O You melting God in your union with Your love, O You resting God on my breasts, without You I cannot exist.

I, 18. God compares the Soul to five things
O you lovely rose among the thorns, O you hovering bee in the honey, O you pure dove in your being, O you beautiful sun in your radiance, O you full moon in your place in the heavens, I cannot turn away from you.

I, 19. God woos the Soul in six ways
You are my softest pillow, my loveliest bed,[7] my most intimate resting-place, my deepest desire, my highest honour! You are a delight to my Godhead, a thirst for my humanity, a stream for my ardour!

I, 20. The Soul praises God in return in six ways
You are my mirror mountain, a feast for my eyes, a loss of myself, a storm in my heart, a defeat and a renunciation of my power, my greatest security!

I, 21. Of knowledge and of pleasure
Love without knowledge is darkness to the wise soul, knowledge without pleasure is the torment of Hell to her, pleasure without death she cannot lament enough.

I, 22. Of the message of St Mary and how one virtue follows another and how the Soul was made in the *jubilus*[8] of the Trinity and how St Mary suckled all the saints and still does
The sweet dew of the uncreated Trinity has fallen from the fountain of the eternal Godhead into the flower of the chosen maid and the fruit of this flower is an immortal God and a mortal man and a living hope of eternal life, and Our Redeemer has become Bridegroom.[9]

---

7   The 'bed of love' is a recurrent image in the *FL*. Cf. I, 22 (p. 31); I, 44 (p. 35); II, 2 (p. 38); III, 9 (p. 60); V, 34 (p. 101); VII, 21 (p. 128).
8   In mystical writings of the thirteenth century the Latin term *jubilus* denoted the ecstatic state of the soul when released from earthly constraints. Here it is used to describe the state of the Trinity when the human soul is created.
9   For an analysis of the associative significance and poetic resonance of the image of dew in Mechthild's writings, see Michel (1986: 510ff.).

The Bride has become intoxicated in the contemplation of the noble countenance:

In the supreme power she loses herself, in the most radiant light she is herself blind and in the greatest blindness she sees most clearly. In the greatest clarity she is both dead and alive.

The longer she is dead, the more happily she lives.

The more happily she lives, the more she learns.

The less she becomes, the more flows to her.

The more she is afraid, . . .[10]

The richer she becomes, the poorer she is.

The more deeply she lives (in God), the more outspread she is.[11]

. . ., the more forbearing she is.

The deeper her wounds become, the more she rages.

The more loving God is towards her, the higher she soars.

The more radiantly she is illumined by the Godhead, the closer she comes to it.

The more she strives, the more peacefully she rests.

. . ., the more she understands.

The quieter she is, the louder she cries out.

. . ., the more she works wonders with His strength from within herself.

The more His desire grows, the greater their wedding becomes.

The narrower the bed[12] becomes, the closer the embrace.

The sweeter the kisses taste on the lips, the more lovingly they look at one another.

The more painfully they part, the more He gives her.

The more she consumes, the more she has.

The more humbly she takes her leave, the sooner she returns.

The warmer she stays, the more readily she sparks.

The more she burns, the brighter she glows.

The more God's praise is increased, the greater her desire becomes.

Ah, where did our Redeemer become Bridegroom? In the *jubilus* of the Holy Trinity; when God could no longer contain Himself, He

---

10 The ellipsis points denote lacunae in the text of this chapter.

11 Neumann (1993: 15, n. I, 22, 17) notes that the description of the soul's experience in dimensional symbolism has its origins in the Old Testament (cf. Ephesians 3: 18 and Psalm 118: 22).

12 Cf. p. 30, n. 7.

made the Soul and, out of great love, gave Himself to her as her own. 'Of what are you made, Soul, that you rise so high above all creatures and mingle with the Holy Trinity and yet remain wholly yourself?' 'You have spoken of my beginning, now I shall tell you truthfully: I was made in that same place[13] by Love and that is why no creature can assure me of my noble nature nor detract from it, save Love alone.' 'Blessed Mary, dear Lady, you are the mother of this wonder. When did this happen to you?' 'When the *jubilus* of Our Father was so distressed by Adam's fall that He could not but be angry, then the eternal wisdom of the almighty Godhead used me to check this anger. Then the Father chose me to be a bride so that He might have something to love, for His dear Bride, the noble Soul, was dead; and then the Son chose me to be a mother and the Holy Spirit received me as a lover. Then I alone was the Bride of the Holy Trinity and Mother of the orphans and brought them before the eyes of God so that they might not all completely sink, as some of them had done. When I thus became the Mother of many a homeless child, my breasts became full of the pure, undefiled milk of true, bountiful mercy, so that I suckled the prophets and the wise men before I was born. After that I suckled Jesus in my childhood; furthermore, in my youth I suckled God's Bride, holy Christianity, by the cross, where I became so desolate and wretched when the sword of Jesus' physical pain sliced spiritually into my soul.' Then both His wounds and her breasts were open; the wounds poured, the breasts flowed, so that the Soul was revived and wholly restored when He poured the pure red wine into her red mouth. When the Soul was thus born out of the open wounds and became alive, then she was childlike and very young. If she was to recover fully after her death and birth, then God's Mother had to be her mother and wet-nurse; this was and is very fitting, for God is her rightful Father and she His rightful Bride, and she is in all her being like Him. 'Lady, in your old age you suckled the holy Apostles with your maternal teaching and your powerful prayer, so that God honoured them as you wished. Lady, thus you suckled and still suckle the hearts of martyrs with strong faith, the ears of confessors with holy protection, virgins with your chastity, widows with constancy, married people with magnanimity, sinners with patience. Lady, now you must suckle us, for your breasts are still so full that you will not dry up. If you no longer wished to give suck then you would be in great pain, for truly I have seen your breasts so full that

---

[13] That is, the Trinity.

seven jets shot simultaneously from one of your breasts over my body and over my soul. At that time you took from me a burden which no friend of God may carry without heartfelt sorrow. And so you should continue to give suck until the Day of Judgement; then you will be drained, for by then the children of God and your children will be weaned and grown fully into eternal life. Ah, after that we shall know and see in boundless delight the milk and those same breasts too that Jesus kissed so often.

I, 23. You should pray that God may love you deeply, often and long, for then you would become pure, beautiful and holy
Ah Lord, love me deeply and love me often and love me long! For the more deeply You love me, the purer I shall be, the more often You love me, the more beautiful I shall be, the longer You love me, the more holy I shall be here on Earth.

I, 24. How God answers the Soul
That I love you deeply is because of my nature, for I myself am Love. That I love you often is because of my desire, for I long to be loved deeply. That I love you long is because of my eternal nature for I am without end and without beginning.

I, 35. The desert has twelve things
You should love nothingness
You should flee somethingness
You should stand alone
And should go to no one.
You should not be too busy
And should stand free of all things.
You should release the bound
And restrain the free.
You should tend the sick
And yet have no care for yourself.
You should drink of the water of suffering
And light the fire of love with the kindling of virtue:
Then you will live in the true desert.

I, 44. Of the path of love in seven things, of three bridal garments and of dancing
'Ah, loving Soul, do you want to know what your path might be like?' 'Yes, dear Holy Spirit, tell me about it.' 'When you have gone beyond the distress of repentance and beyond the pain of confession and

beyond the labour of penance and beyond the love of the world and beyond the temptation of the devil and beyond the luxury of the flesh and beyond accursed self-will, that acts as such a drag on many a soul that they never reach true love, and when you have defeated all your greatest enemies, then you will be so tired that you say: "Handsome Young Man, I desire You, where shall I find You?" Then the Young Man says: "I hear a voice that has something of the sound of love. Many is the day that I have wooed her with no response. Now I am moved, I must go to her. She is the one who bears both distress and love together."' In the sweet dew of the morning, that is, the restrained fervour that enters the Soul first, her chamberlains, the five Senses, say: 'Lady, you should dress yourself.' 'My dear ones, where am I going?' 'Truly, we have heard a whisper that the Prince will come to you in the dew and in the lovely birdsong. Ah, Lady, now don't take too long!' And so she puts on an underslip of gentle humility and the humility is such that she cannot bear anything under it; over that a white dress of pure chastity and the purity is such that she cannot bear any thoughts, words or caresses that might sully her. Then she wraps herself in a cloak of holy reputation, which she has adorned with every virtue. Then she goes into the company of holy people in the forest; there the very sweetest nightingale sings of the harmonious union with God day and night and she hears a number of sweet voices there from the birds of holy knowledge. Still the Young Man did not arrive. Now she sends out messengers, for she wants to dance, and she sent for the faith of Abraham and for the longing of the Prophets and for the chaste humility of Our Lady, St Mary, and for all the holy virtues of Our Lord Jesus Christ and for all the goodness of His chosen ones.[14] And so a marvellous dance of praise takes place there. Then the Young Man comes to her and says: 'Young Lady, you should dance, following faithfully the steps my chosen ones have demonstrated to you.' Then she says: 'I cannot dance, Lord, unless You lead me. If You want me to dance with spring in my step, then You must lead me in with Your singing; then I shall spring into love, from love into knowledge, from knowledge into pleasure, from pleasure into what is beyond all human senses. That is where I would like to stay and yet I want to spiral even higher.' And the Young Man has to sing the following: 'Through me into you and through you from me.' 'Happy with You, wretched away from You!'

---

[14] In the course of the description of the soul's path in love, the tense shifts between the report in the preterite tense and the immediacy of the present tense.

Then the Young Man says: 'Young Lady, you have performed this dance of praise well, you shall have your way with the Virgin's son, for now you are tired through love. Come at midday to the shadow of the fountain, to the bed of love,[15] there you shall refresh yourself with Him.' Then the young Lady says: 'O Lord, it is too much that she, who has no love in herself unless first stirred by You, is Your partner in love.' Then the Soul speaks to the Senses, who are her chamberlains: 'Now I am a little tired of dancing, leave me, I must go to where I can refresh myself.' Then the Senses say to the Soul: 'Lady, if you were to refresh yourself in the tears of love shed by Mary Magdalene, you would very likely find satisfaction there.' The Soul: 'Be quiet, sirs, you don't fully understand what I mean! Leave me in peace, for a while I want to drink of the wine that is unadulterated.'[16] 'Lady, great love is at hand in the chastity of virgins.' 'That may well be, but that is not the most important thing about me.' 'You could refresh yourself in the blood of the martyrs.' 'I have suffered martyrdom on so many occasions that I cannot go that way now.' 'Pure people like to live in the counsel of the confessors.' 'I will always hold to counsel, both in what I do and in what I don't do, but I can't go there now.' 'In the wisdom of the Apostles you will find great security.' 'I have wisdom here with me, I shall always choose the best with that.' 'Lady, the angels are bright and beautiful in the colour of love; if you wish to refresh yourself, then ascend to them.' 'The bliss of the angels makes me ache with love if I don't see their Lord and my Bridegroom.' 'Then refresh yourself in the holy austere life which God gave to John the Baptist.' 'I am prepared for pain, however, the strength of love exceeds all effort.' 'Lady, if you wish to refresh yourself with love, then bow down to the small Child in the lap of the Virgin and see and taste how the joy of the angels sucked the supernatural milk from the eternal Maid.' 'Suckling and cradling a child is a childlike love. I am a fully grown bride, I want to go to my Love.' 'O Lady, if you go there, then we shall be completely blinded, for the Godhead, as you well know, is so fiery hot that all the fire and incandescence, in which Heaven and all the saints burn and glow, streams from His divine breath and out of His human mouth on the advice of the Holy Spirit. How could you last even an hour there?' 'The fish cannot drown in water, the bird cannot sink in the air, gold may not be destroyed in the fire, for it is there that it acquires its

---

15 Cf. p. 30, n. 7.
16 Cf. II, 24 (p. 45); III, 3 (p. 57).

brightness and lustrous colour. God has granted all creatures that they live according to their nature; I must leave all things to go to God, who is my Father by nature, my Brother in His humanity, my Bridegroom in love and I His bride eternally. So how then could I resist my nature?[17] Do you imagine that I cannot feel Him?[18] He can both burn with ardour and cool with comfort. Now don't be too distressed! You shall still advise me; when I return, I shall be in need of your guidance, for this Earth is full of snares.' And so the most dear goes to the most handsome in the secret chambers of the invisible Godhead. There she finds the bed of love[19] and the room of love made ready, not in a human way, by God. Then Our Lord says: 'Stop, Lady Soul!' 'What is Your command, Lord?' 'You should undress yourself!' 'Lord, what will happen to me then?' 'Lady Soul, you have so much of my nature that between you and me there can be nothing. Never was an angel so honoured that he was granted for one hour what is given to you eternally. Thus, you should strip yourself of both fear and shame and all external virtues; only those which are innate should you nurture eternally: that is your noble longing and your boundless desire. These I shall satisfy eternally with my infinite generosity.' 'Lord, now I am a naked soul and You in Yourself a richly adorned God. Our communion together is eternal life without death.' Then a blessed stillness follows that they both desire. He gives Himself to her and she herself to Him. What may happen to her now, she knows, and I comfort myself with that. Now this cannot last long; where two lovers come together secretly, they must often leave one another without separating.

Dear friend of God, I have written down this path of love for you, may God favour your heart with it! Amen.

---

[17] Mechthild's description of God as her Father 'by nature' appears to have aroused controversy to which she replies in VI, 31 (p. 115).
[18] In the translation of this problematic sentence in the original text I have followed Neumann's conjecture (1993: 25f., n. I, 44, 74f.).
[19] Cf. p. 30, n. 7.

Book II

The lyrical, mystical tone of Book I is continued in songs of love (II, 2; II, 5; II, 6; II, 17–18) and exchanges (II, 21) between God and the Soul. However, the individuality of Mechthild's prophetic voice also emerges more clearly in her fully-fledged vision of John the Baptist (II, 4) celebrating Mass. Mechthild aligns herself with a number of saints and figures from the New Testament, juxtaposing and fusing events from salvation history with her personal history in a narrative of complex temporal perspectives (II, 24).

Mechthild's contemporaries have a greater presence in this book, in her identification of her enemies as those who are false in the religious life. There is also a greater awareness of a critical readership. Mechthild expresses her anxiety about the reception of her writings (II, 26), but defends herself by invoking the 'call to write' topos. She reports how God appeared to her and left her, and by extension her readers, in no doubt that He is the inspiration, the source and indeed the very author of her words. Mechthild's writings are to be understood within that exegetical tradition which stems from the metaphorical interpretation of the Bible as the Book of God's Word. Mechthild's expression of a sense of personal inadequacy and unworthiness is to become one of the most characteristic features of her self-projection in her text. God's reassurance places her within the hagiographical tradition of *sancta simplicitas* ['holy simplicity'], in which the emphasis on the holy person's lack of formal education and their reliance on the Holy Spirit serves to authenticate their experiences and, of course, to disarm potential opponents. In the course of her book Mechthild uses this concept polemically to legitimise her writings and to justify her criticism of those who are 'book learned'.

II, 2. Of two songs of love about Him who was seen in love
I would gladly die of love
If I could;
I have seen
With my bright eyes
Him whom I love
Standing in my soul.
The bride who has taken her Lover in

Does not need to go far.
Love cannot easily disappear
Where the young lady keeps seeking out the Young Man.
His noble nature is always ready
To receive her eagerly again
And to draw her close to His heart.
This may well elude the foolish
Who are unwilling to pursue their Love.

'O noble Eagle, o sweet Lamb, o fiery Glow, set me on fire!
How long must I be parched like this?
One hour is too much for me,
One day seems a thousand years to me,
When You choose to be distant from me;
If this were to last eight days
I would prefer to go to Hell
– Where indeed I am already –
Rather than that God be distant from the loving Soul;
That is a pain greater than mortal death
And greater than all the torments of Hell, believe me!
The nightingale cannot help but always sing,
For it is her nature to give voice to love;
Should anyone take that from her, she would be dead.
Ah mighty Lord, take heed of my distress!'

Then the Holy Spirit spoke to the Soul: 'Ah noble young lady, get yourself ready, your Lover is coming.' Then she started and rejoiced inwardly and said: 'Ah dear messenger, would it were always so! I am so unworthy and so very inconstant that I know no peace away from my Lover. Whenever I feel that His love is becoming cooler then I ache all over and I know that, wretched, I must go after Him.' Then the messenger said: 'You should cleanse yourself and pour water on yourself and prepare a bed[20] and scatter flowers.' Then the desolate Soul said: 'When I cleanse myself, I cannot help but be ashamed, when I pour water on myself, I cannot help but cry, when I prepare a bed, I cannot help but hope, when I pluck flowers then I cannot help but love. When my Lord comes, then I am transported out of myself because the sound of the strings He brings me is so sweet that it dispels all the urges of my flesh, and the music of His strings is so full of sweetness that it dispels all the sorrow of my heart.'

---

[20] Cf. p. 30, n. 7.

II, 4. Of the poor maid, of the Mass of John the Baptist, of the transubstantiation of the host into the Lamb, of the beauty of the angels, of four kinds of holy people and of the golden penny[21]

When a poor maid was unable to attend Mass because she was unfortunately not well enough to serve Our Lord, He revealed to her how useful it may be for a person to be of good will, even if they cannot act themselves. Then this is how she spoke to God: 'Ah, my dear Lord, am I to go without Mass today?'

In this state of plaintive longing, God took from her all her earthly senses and brought her in a wondrous way into a beautiful church, in which she found no one. Then she thought to herself: Oh no, you wretched sluggard, now you've arrived too late; that you have at last got yourself out of bed isn't going to help you much here. Then she saw a young man arrive, carrying a bunch of white flowers which he scattered beneath the tower and then left. Then another came, carrying a bunch of violets that he scattered in the middle of the church. Then yet another came, carrying a bunch of roses, which he scattered decoratively before the altar of Our Lady. Then the fourth came, carrying a bunch of white lilies and scattered them in the choir. When they had done this, they bowed gracefully and departed. These young men were so noble and pleasing to look at that no one's suffering could be so great that it would not vanish, were they to contemplate them. Then two pupils dressed in white appeared, carrying two lights that they placed upon the altar; then they moved away gracefully and remained in the choir.

Then a fairly tall man arrived who was emaciated but not very old; his clothes were so thin that you could see his arms and legs through them. He was carrying a white lamb at his breast and two lamps hanging from his fingers. Then he went up to the altar and placed the lamb on it and bowed lovingly. This was John the Baptist; he was to sing the Mass. Then a young man, who was very gentle in his demeanour, arrived, holding an eagle to his breast; this was John the Evangelist. Then a simple man, St Peter, arrived. Then a strong young man arrived, carrying a bundle of vestments with which they robed themselves. Then a great crowd arrived, this was the mighty company of Heaven, and they filled the church so full that the poor maid could find nowhere to stand.

Then she went to stand below the tower where she found a number

---

[21] For an analysis of this vision see Poor (2000b).

of people dressed in white who had no hair; they had, however, simple crowns on their heads. These were people who had not lived according to the law. They were bereft of the adornment of hair, that is good deeds. How had they got to Heaven then? Through repentance and good will at the time of their death. Further on she found people who were even more beautiful, dressed in violet-coloured clothes; they were adorned with the beautiful hair of virtue and crowned with God's law. Then she found people who were even more beautiful, dressed in rose-coloured clothes; they bore the lovely mark of the widow and a crown of voluntary chastity.

The poor maid was dressed shabbily and was physically weak and could not stay among these three groups. Then she went to stand in front of the choir and looked in to where Our Lady stood in the highest place, together with St Catherine, Cecilia, bishops, martyrs, angels and very many virgins. When this poor person saw this great company, then she looked at herself to see if she dared stay, given her pitiful state. Then she had a cloak of red brown cloth around her that had been made by Love to reflect the burning of her senses for God and for all good things. The cloak was adorned with gold and also with a song that went like this: 'I would gladly die of love.'[22] She saw herself as a noble young lady wearing a chaplet of magnificent gold, inscribed with another song that went like this: 'His eyes into my eyes, his heart into my heart, his soul into my soul, tirelessly embraced.' And her face looked like that of the angels. 'Alas, wretched quagmire[23] that I am, what has happened to me now? I really am not so fortunate as I have seen myself there.' All those who were in the choir looked at her with a sweet smile. Then Our Lady motioned to her to stand above Catherine; then she went to stand by Our dear Lady for it was a rare opportunity for her to see and speak to the Mother of God: 'Ah, you dear and gracious Lady!' She thought it a blessing that the unworthy crow might stand next to the noble turtledove. All those in the choir were arrayed in lustrous gold and were caught up in soaring bliss, brighter than the sun.

Then they began the Mass as follows: *Gaudeamus omnes in*

---

[22] This is the first line of the love song (II, 2) which precedes this chapter in Book II.

[23] This is a recurrent image in Mechthild's description of herself. The Middle High German word is 'phuol' and can mean puddle, mudhole, quagmire, marshland, swampland, morass. I have chosen to translate this rather difficult image consistently as (quag)mire.

domino,[24] and at every mention of the name of Our Lady she genuflected while the others bowed, because God had given her the greatest honour. Then this wretch, who had come to the Mass, said: 'Ah Lady, if only I might now receive the Body of God, for there is nothing to be afraid of here.' Then the Mother of God said: 'Yes, dear girl, make your confession!' Then the Queen of Heaven beckoned to John the Evangelist; he went out and heard the sinner's confession. Then she asked him to tell her how long she had to live. Then John said: 'I cannot tell you because God does not wish it; for if the time were long, then you might become depressed because of your many troubles; however, if the time were short, you might fall to wishing for a long life because of the distress in your heart.'

Then John went to read the Gospel, the *Liber generationis*.[25] Then the wretch spoke to Our Lady: 'Should I put something in the offertory box?' Then Our Lady said: 'Yes, as long as you won't take it away from Him again.' Then the wretch said: 'Ah Lady, you must grant me this grace from God.' Then Our Lady said: 'Now take this golden penny, that is: your own self-will, and offer it to my noble Son in all things.' The little person took the large penny with great reverence and holy fear. Then she examined how the coin had been minted. On one side of the penny was shown Christ being taken down from the cross, on the other was all the Kingdom of Heaven with the nine choirs and God's throne at the top. Then God's voice spoke to her: 'If you make me an offering of this penny and have no intention of taking it back, then I will take you down from the cross and fetch you to me in my kingdom.'

After this, that same priest, who was ordained in his mother's womb by the Holy Spirit, celebrated a low Mass.[26] When he took the white wafer in his hands, that same lamb, that had been on the altar, stood up and, as the priest spoke and gestured with his hands, the lamb merged into the wafer and the wafer merged into the lamb, so that I no longer saw the wafer, only a lamb covered in blood hanging on a red cross. I shall never ever be able to forget those sweet eyes with which it looked upon us. Then the poor maid appealed to Our dear Lady as follows: 'Ah dear Mother, pray to your exalted Son that He might give Himself to me, poor wretch that I am.' Then she saw

---

[24] 'Let us all rejoice in the Lord'. These are the first words of the introit for the Feast of the Blessed Virgin Mary of Good Counsel, celebrated on the 26th day of April.

[25] The 'Book of Generation' is the listing of Jesus Christ's genealogy in Matthew 1: 1–16.

[26] That is a simpler form of the Mass ritual, in contradistinction to 'high Mass'.

how a bright ray of light shone out of Our Lady's mouth onto the altar and touched the lamb with her prayer so that God Himself spoke out of the lamb: 'Mother, I will gladly put myself in the place that you wish me to.' Then the poor maid went to the altar with great love and with an open soul. Then St John took the white lamb with its red wounds and placed it in her mouth between her jaws. Then the pure lamb settled itself on its own image in her stable and suckled at her heart with its sweet mouth. The more it suckled, the more she gave it. [Now she to whom this happened is dead and has departed this life. May God help us to see her again in the host of angels! Amen.][27]

II, 5. A song of the Soul to God about five things, and how God is a garment of the Soul and the Soul a garment of God

'You shine into my soul
As the sun does on gold.
Whenever I may rest in You, Lord,
Then my delight is manifold.
You clothe Yourself with my soul
And You are also her most intimate garment.
That there must be a parting,
Truly, I have never experienced greater heartache!
If You were to love me more
Then I would most assuredly depart from here
For where I might love You freely and unceasingly.
Now I have sung to You,
But I have not succeeded;
If You were to sing to me
Then I would succeed.'

II, 6. In response God sings of five things in the Soul

'When I shine, then you must sparkle;
When I flow, then you must be flooded.
When you sigh, then you draw my divine heart into you,
When you cry for me
Then I take you in my arms
But when you love, then we two become one,

---

[27] These final two sentences appear in the Einsiedeln manuscript as part of the transcription of the text into Alemannic and they also appear in the *Ld*. However, it is unclear whether these sentences were added first to the *FL* and then to the *Ld* or whether they were added to the *Ld* and then to the *FL* as part of a later comparative revision of both texts. See Neumann (1993: 32, n. II, 4, 102f.).

And when we two are one,
Then there can never be a parting,
But rather there is a delightful expectation
Between the pair of us.'
'Lord, then I await with hunger and with thirst,
With hounding and with longing
That joyful hour
When out of Your divine mouth
The chosen words flow
That are heard by no one
Other than the Soul alone,
That divests herself of the Earth
And places her ear by Your mouth.
Yes, she grasps the find of love!'

II, 17. How God woos the Soul and makes her wise in His love

This is how God woos the artless Soul and makes her wise in His love: 'Ah, dear dove, your feet are red, your feathers smooth, your mouth is well formed, your eyes are beautiful, your head is sleek, your movement delightful, your flight swift and you return all too quickly to Earth.'

II, 18. How the Soul interprets God's wooing in eight things

Lord, my feet are stained with the blood of Your true act of redemption, my feathers have been smoothed by Your noble favour, my mouth has been formed by Your Holy Spirit, my eyes transfigured by Your fiery light, my head is made sleek by Your faithful protection, my movement is delightful because of Your generous gift, my flight is made swift by Your restless desire, my sinking back to Earth is because of Your union with my body. The more You free me, the longer I may hover in You.

II, 21. If you wish to see the mountain then you must have seven things

I have seen a mountain,
It all happened very quickly,
For no body could bear it,
Were the soul there for an hour.
The foot of the mountain was cloudy white
And the top bright as the fiery sun.
I could see
Neither the beginning nor end of it,

And within itself, like the colour of molten gold,
It shone in ineffable love.
Then I said: 'Lord, blessed are the eyes
That may gaze upon this flowing love forever
And bear witness to this wonder;
I shall never be able to give it expression!'
Then the Mountain said: 'The eyes that would see me in this
way
Must be graced with seven things, for there is no other way
they may be favoured.
These are: to borrow reluctantly, to pay back willingly
And to keep nothing for yourself,
To meet enmity with goodness and violence with love
To be free of guilt and ready to receive.'

II, 24. How the loving Soul keeps company with God and with His chosen ones and how she shall be the equal of all the saints. How the Devil and the Soul talk together

Ah Lord Jesus Christ, Your innocent suffering comforts me, because in all my suffering I am guilty, and Your redemptive death keeps You present to me, and Your undefiled blood has flowed through my soul.

Mary, dear Mother, I stand by the cross with you with all my Christian faith, and the sword of holy suffering cuts through my soul, because of the inconstancy of so many who appear to be religious.

John the Baptist, I have been taken prisoner with you because the unfaithful maid of falsehood has killed God's word in my mouth.[28]

John the Evangelist, in heartfelt love I have fallen asleep with you on the breast of Jesus Christ, and then seen and heard such marvellous wonders that my body has often been bereft of its senses.[29]

Peter, I have been crucified with you because I shall never be at ease in my human condition, and spiritually I often ache for the praise of Jesus Christ.

Paul, I have been so wondrously caught up with you[30] and have seen such a dwelling place that nothing has ever astonished me more than that I have survived this. When I think of how the Heavenly Father is there the blessed cup-bearer and Jesus the cup, the Holy

---

[28] Cf. Matthew 14: 1–12 and Mark 6: 14–29.
[29] In the Middle Ages John the Apostle was the preferred saint in mystical circles, particularly in the convents, but also amongst Dominicans. Cf. Schmidt (1995: 361f., n. 77) and John 13: 23.
[30] Cf. 2 Corinthians 12: 2–4.

Spirit the pure wine and how together the Trinity is the full cup, and Love the powerful mistress in charge of the wine cellar,[31] then, God knows, were Love to invite me into that house, I would accept with such alacrity. However, I will now drink gall here willingly. Ah dear Jesus, may You now reward lovingly those who pour out bitterness for me here, for they make me rich in grace. I was given a cup of gall that was so strong that it penetrated all of my body and soul. Then I prayed to God for that person in particular who had poured me out this cup, that He might pour out heavenly wine for him. And indeed, He did that and said: 'Noble maid, be of good cheer! The greatness of my wonder shall come over you, lions shall fear you, bears shall obey you, wolves shall flee you, the lamb shall be your companion.' I am sure, as has been the case until now, that I shall have to drain many a cup of gall, for, unfortunately, the Devil has many cup-bearers amongst religious people, who are so full of poison, that they cannot drink it alone, but must pour it out in bitterness for God's children.

Stephen,[32] I kneel beside you before Jewish hearts among the sharp stones, for large and small they rain down on me. Those who appear to be good people stone me from behind and run away and do not want me to know that they have done this to me; but God has seen it.

Lawrence,[33] I was bound with you for more than twenty years on a dreadful gridiron; however, God preserved me unscathed and released me over seven years ago now.

Martin,[34] I live with you in obscurity and true love of God has martyred me more than all trials and tribulations.

Dominic,[35] my dear father, I have something in common with you, for I have longed many a day that the sinful blood of my heart might flow under the feet of faithless heretics.

---

[31] Cf. III, 3 (p. 56).

[32] Cf. Acts 7: 54–60. Magdeburg had the relics of St Stephen, which had been brought from Mainz in 980 by Bishop Hildewart. Cf. Ancelet-Hustache (1926: 205).

[33] Lawrence was the patron saint of a monastery that was founded in Magdeburg in 1209. Cf. Ancelet-Hustache (1926: 205).

[34] Martin (316/35–397), born in Hungary, became Bishop of Tours and a patron saint of France. He was one of the most popular saints in the Middle Ages.

[35] From 1206 till 1214 Dominic preached in southern France amongst the heretical groups of Waldensians, Albigensians and Cathars (see Introduction, p. 7, n. 30). His successor, Jordan of Saxony, reported the threat posed to Dominic by these heretics.

Catherine,[36] I go into battle with you, for the masters of Hell wanted to strike me down. One of them came to me as beautiful as a sunbeam, so that I should think he was an angel, and he brought with him a luminous book and said: 'Take this kiss of peace when you cannot get to Mass.'[37] Then the Soul spoke with disciplined wisdom: 'He who knows no peace himself cannot give me peace.' Then he left and transformed himself and came again in the guise of a very poor, sick man, whose innards were falling out, and said: 'Ah, you are so holy, heal me.' The Soul, however, then said: 'Whoever is sick himself can heal no one.' 'It is written: Whoever has more to give, should help the other.' 'It is also written: One should help no one against God.' 'To do good is not to act against God.' 'Where there is no good in something, one can do no good. You have an everlasting sickness;[38] if you wish to recover, then go and present yourself to a priest or a bishop or an archbishop or the pope.[39] I have no power other than to sin.' Then he spoke in fury: 'I shall never do that.' Then he fumed darkly and behaved boorishly and left. But I am not afraid of him.[40]

Mary Magdalene,[41] I live with you in the wilderness, for all things are alien to me except God alone.

Lord heavenly Father, there is an indefinable breath that moves constantly between You and me, in which I witness and see many wonders and inexpressible things, but unfortunately this does me little good, because I am such a weak vessel, that I cannot bear even Your smallest spark. Unbound Love lives in the Senses, for it is still entangled in earthly things and so a person may cry out: 'Love in

[36] From his stay at the court of Friedrich II Archbishop Albrecht brought back one of St Catherine's fingers as a holy relic to Magdeburg around 1220. Catherine became the second patron saint of the cathedral. Cf. Ancelet-Hustache (1926: 205).

[37] The word in the text, *petze*, is a corruption of the Latin *pax* [peace] and refers to the mutual greeting of the faithful in the eucharistic liturgy as a sign of their love and union. Originally an actual kiss, the form of the Peace has been modified in all rites. In this context it refers to the object (perhaps a crucifix or an image of Christ) which the celebrant passed around to be kissed.

[38] Cf. Jeremiah 30: 12.

[39] Cf. Matthew 8: 4

[40] The dialogue between Mechthild and the Devil is reminiscent of Christ's temptation in the wilderness. Cf. Matthew 4: 1–10; Mark 1: 12–13; Luke 4: 1–13. Cf. a further dialogue Mechthild has with a devil in IV, 2 (p. 71f.).

[41] Schmidt (1995: 367, n. 83) draws attention to an account in the *Legenda aurea* [The golden legend] of how Mary Magdalene was nourished by God while she was in the desert.

grace is remote from the Senses and has not yet, unfortunately, conquered the Soul.'[42] Many people have fallen because their soul remained unwounded.[43] Solomon and David received the Holy Spirit in their human senses; however, when their senses were changed, then they fell into false love. God knows, their souls had not sunk into the most profound depths below all creatures,[44] nor were they wounded by that powerful part of love; for he who has never drunk of the best wine is often the most raucous. Bound Love lives in the Soul and rises above human senses and does not allow the Body its own will; it is restrained and very calm; it folds its wings and listens for the ineffable voice and looks into the incomprehensible light and with great eagerness strives to accomplish the will of the Lord. If the Body is able to flap its wings, then the Soul may never experience the most sublime that is accessible to mankind. In this bound love, the wounded Soul grows rich and her external senses very poor, for the more wealth God finds in her, the more deeply she humbles herself in the true nobility of love. Whenever a person has been bound by the source of this powerful love I can find in them no falling into mortal sin, for when the Soul is bound, it can only love. May God bind us all in this way!

II, 26. Of this book and the scribes of this book

I was warned about this book and people told me that if it were not protected, it could be thrown on the fire. Then I did as I have done since I was a child; whenever I was distressed then I had to pray. Then I turned in prayer to my Love and said: 'Ah Lord, now I am distressed because of Your honour; if You do not comfort me now, then You have misled me, for You ordered me to write it Yourself.' Then God revealed Himself at once to my sorrowful soul and held this book in His right hand and said: 'My love, do not be too distressed, no one may burn the truth. Anyone who would take it from my hand would have to be stronger than me. This book is three-fold and signifies me alone. This parchment, which encloses it, signifies my pure, white and just humanity that suffered death for your sake. The words signify my wondrous Godhead; they flow hour by hour into your soul out of my divine mouth. The tone of the words

---

[42] In Mechthild's concept of 'bound' and 'unbound' love Schmidt (1995: 363, n. 85 and n. 87) detects the mediated influence of Richard of St Victor's tract *De quattuor gradibus violentiae caritatis* [On the four steps of violent love].

[43] That is, by love.

[44] Cf. IV, 12 (pp. 74ff.).

signifies my living spirit and through this the full truth is realised. Now look into all these words, how gloriously they reveal my mystery and do not doubt yourself!'

'Ah Lord, if I were an educated, religious man and You had worked this singular, great wonder in him, then You would have had eternal honour from that. Now, how can anyone believe of You that You have built a golden house in a filthy quagmire[45] and really live there with Your mother and with all creatures and with Your entire heavenly host? Lord, the wisdom of this world cannot find You in this.'

'Daughter, many a wise man, through carelessness, loses on a broad highway the precious gold with which he wanted to go to a school of advanced studies; someone will find it. My nature has often led me to seek out the lowliest, humblest, most hidden place whenever I granted special favour; the highest mountains on Earth may not receive the revelation of my grace, for the current of my Holy Spirit flows naturally down to the valley. One finds many a wise master versed in scripture, who is, however, a fool in my eyes. And what is more: With regard to them, it is a great honour to me and it strengthens holy Christianity considerably that the untutored mouth, inspired by the Holy Spirit, instructs the learned tongue.'[46]

'Ah, Lord, I sigh and wish and beg on behalf of Your scribes, who have copied this book, that You might also grant them, as a reward, grace such as was never bestowed on man; for, Lord, there is a thousand times more of Your gift than of Your creatures who might receive it.' Then Our Lord said; 'They have written it in golden letters, and so all the words of this book shall be on their outer clothes, forever visible in my kingdom; they shall be written in heavenly lustrous gold on top of all their splendour, for love that is freely given must always be the greatest thing about a person.'

While Our Lord was saying this to me, I saw the marvellous truth in eternal splendour. Ah Lord, I beg you to protect this book from the eyes of false vigilance, for that has come amongst us from Hell; it never came out of Heaven. It was engendered in Lucifer's heart and born in spiritual arrogance and puffed up in hatred and has grown so big in mighty rage, that it believes no virtue to be its equal. And so the children of God must be oppressed and allow themselves to be humiliated if they wish to attain the highest honour with Jesus. We

---

45 Cf. p. 40, n. 23.
46 Cf. Matthew 11: 26 and Luke 10: 21–22.

must at all times maintain a holy vigilance to save ourselves from our shortcomings. We should practise a loving vigilance towards our fellow Christians, alerting them to their wrongdoing only in a spirit of good faith; this would save us from much unnecessary talk. Amen.

Book III

The profile of Book III is dominated by the visions of Heaven (III, 1), Purgatory (III, 15) and Hell (III, 21). In Mechthild's grand vision of Heaven, time is overcome in a resolution of the linearity of salvation history within the circularity of mystical union. Mechthild's visionary experience also takes her to that moment before time existed in the account of the Soul's creation and her mystical relationship with God (III, 9). Hell is conceived principally as a negative inversion of Heaven. Purgatory, the most frequent eschatological location in medieval visionary literature, is the most common site of Mechthild's visionary experience. It is in the contiguity of the temporal and the eternal world of Purgatory that the interface between God and Mechthild on the one hand and Mechthild and her contemporaries on the other is most clearly expressed.

The two principal modes of expression employed by Mechthild are an ecstatic-mystical voice, which communicates the love relationship between the Soul and its Creator, and an authoritative prophetic voice, which teaches, admonishes and encourages contemporaries.[47] The fundamental paradigm for the first voice is the Song of Songs and for the second it is the Psalter.[48] Attention is drawn to the intertextual relationship between Mechthild's writings and these two biblical books in the address to the Bride of the Song of Songs in III, 3 and the citing of David and Solomon as two of the five prophets who 'illumine' her book (III, 20).

In the two previous books, references to her contemporaries had been couched in general terms. They were either fellow 'loving souls', whom Mechthild instructs about the path to mystical union, or they were 'imperfect religious people', who are hostile towards her and critical of her writings. In Book III, Mechthild is more specific about the circles within which she moves. She identifies herself as a beguine (III, 15) and her high regard for the Dominicans becomes evident in her vision of their reward in Heaven, although they are not immune from her critical eye. The didactic element in

---

47 Cf. Schmidt (1988: 41).
48 Cf. Andersen (2000: 148ff.).

her work emerges clearly in the teaching, imparted to her by the Holy Spirit, which she offers her readership on the nature of false virtues (III, 14).

III, 1. Of the Kingdom of Heaven and the nine choirs and who shall fill the gap. Of the throne of the Apostles and St Mary and where Christ sits. Of the reward of the preachers, martyrs and virgins and of the unbaptised children[49]

The Soul spoke as follows to her Desire: 'Ah, go and see where my Lover is and tell Him I would make love.' Then Desire went immediately, for it is by nature quick, and came up on high and cried out: 'Great Lord, open up and let me in.' Then the Master of the house said: 'What is it that you want that you're making so much noise?' 'Lord, I have to tell you that my lady can't live much longer like this; if You would flow, then she could swim, for the fish can't survive long on the sand and remain fresh.' 'Go back, I'm not going to let you in now unless you bring to me the hungry Soul whom I desire above all things.' When the messenger returned and the Soul heard the will of her Lord, ah, how she was overcome with delight. She rose up in a gentle swing and in joyful flight. Then two angels came rapidly to meet her; God sent them to her out of deep love, and they said to her: 'Lady Soul, what are you doing so far up? You're still clothed in the darkness of Earth.' Then she said: 'Sirs, just hold your peace and give me a better greeting, I want to go and make love. The closer you sink towards Earth, the more you hide your lovely, heavenly appearance, and the higher I rise, the more brightly I shine.' Then they took the Soul between them and led her happily on. When the Soul saw the land of the angels, where she is known as she truly is, then Heaven was opened to her.

Then she stood there and her heart melted and she looked at her Love and said: 'O Lord, when I look at You I must praise You in wondrous wisdom. Where am I? Am I now lost in You? For I find myself unable to think about the Earth or about any of the sorrows of my heart. It had been my intention, when I should see You, to complain to You greatly about Earth. But, Lord, the sight of You has overcome me, for You have raised me well beyond what I am worth.' Then she knelt down and thanked Him for His grace and took her crown from her head and placed it on the rose-coloured scars on His

---

[49] For an analysis of Mechthild's visions of Heaven and of Hell (III, 21), see Tax (1979).

feet and begged that she might come closer to Him. Then He took her in His divine arms and laid His fatherly hand on her breast and looked into her face. Well, was she kissed at all? In that kiss she was transported up into the highest heights above all the choirs of angels. The greatest wisdom that has ever been made known on this Earth cannot be compared to even the smallest part of the truth that I saw and heard and witnessed there. I saw there things that are unheard of, as my confessors tell me, for I am not educated. Now I fear God, if I remain silent, and yet fear ignorant people, if I write. Most dear people, what can I do about it that this happens to me and has often happened? God has revealed His wonders to me in my humble simplicity and estranged poverty and oppressed shame.

There I saw the creation and the ordering of God's house that He Himself built with His mouth;[50] and in it He has placed what is dearest to Him that He has made with His own hands. The house that has been created is called Heaven, the choirs in it are called the Kingdom, and thus taken together we speak of the Kingdom of Heaven. The composition of the Kingdom of Heaven is finite, but there will never be an end to its existence. Heaven surrounds the choirs, and between Heaven and the beautiful choirs the worldly sinners are ranged, always on much the same level as the choirs so that they might improve and mend their ways. The choirs are so fine and holy and marvellous that no one may enter there without chastity and love and renunciation of all things, for all those who fell from there were holy and so those who wish to enter there must be holy. All unbaptised babies and children up to six years of age fill the gap only as far as the sixth choir. From there as far as the Seraphim, the gap shall be filled by virgins, who sullied themselves with their childish will but never realised the deed and who cleansed themselves afterwards through confession. However, they cannot fully restore themselves, for they have lost their purity. After the Day of Judgement those who are pure spiritual virgins shall fill the gap above the Seraphim, from where Lucifer and those closest to Him were thrown out. Lucifer was guilty simultaneously of three mortal sins: hatred, pride and avarice. These thrust the choir down into the eternal abyss before you could say 'alleluia'. The Kingdom was shocked and all the pillars of Heaven shook. Then a number of others fell.

The void has not yet been filled, there is no one there, and in this

---

[50] That is through an oral command, e.g. 'Let there be light' (Genesis 1: 3).

way it is pure in itself and shines in bliss to honour God. Above the void, God's throne is vaulted with God's might in blooming,[51] shining, fiery brightness and it extends down to the Heaven of the Cherubim, so that God's throne and Heaven form a magnificent dwelling place, and the void and the nine choirs are contained within it. Above God's throne is nothing other than God, God, God, immeasurably great God. Up above on the throne is the mirror of the Godhead, the image of mankind, the light of the Holy Spirit and it is clear how the Three are One God and how they are interlocked. I can say nothing more about this.

John the Baptist shall fill the gap left by Lucifer and shall assume his splendour in the sweet void above the Seraphim, together with all pure spiritual virgins, who are also destined for the void.[52]

By the throne stands Our Lady St Mary; she shall fill no gap, because with her Child she has healed all the wounds of those who afforded themselves grace through their willingness and ability to maintain it. Her Son is God and she a goddess; no one can compare with her.[53] The Apostles live closest of all to God in the throne and have the void amongst the Seraphim as a reward, for they are pure. John the Baptist is also a prince at the throne. The angels dwell no higher than the Seraphim, all above them must be human beings. The holy martyrs and God's preachers and spiritual lovers come into these choirs, even if they are not virgins. Indeed, they come amongst the Cherubim with honour! There, without asking, I saw the reward of the preachers, as it is yet to come about. Their chairs are wonderful, their reward special. The front legs of the chairs are two burning lights, which signify true love and holy example and faithful inner resolve. The back of the chair is so pleasantly free of restraint and in blissful repose so sweet, more than one can express, in contrast to the strict obedience to which they are subject here. Their feet are adorned so beautifully with many precious stones that I would be truly delighted to be given such splendour as a crown. They

---

[51] Cf. p. 28, n. 5.

[52] In the Middle Ages, John the Baptist was regarded as a model of virginity, second only to the Virgin Mary. Amongst the female religious he was held in particular regard. Mechthild accords the 'megde' ['virgins'] the highest position in Heaven after that occupied by the Trinity. Cf. Tax (1979: 121f.) and Ancelet-Hustache (1926: 196ff.).

[53] The Virgin Mary is a goddess in the sense that she has been deified through grace, cf. John 10: 34f. In the same sense, Mechthild refers to the Soul as a 'goddess' (III, 9 [p. 59]) and to the truly religious person as a 'god' (VI, 1 [p. 105]).

have this for the work they have accomplished here on foot. O you preachers, how reluctantly you now set your tongues to work and how unwillingly you turn your ears to the sinner's mouth!

In God's presence I have seen that in the Kingdom of Heaven a breath shall shimmer forth from your mouth and shall rise up out of the choirs to the throne and shall praise the heavenly Father for the wisdom that He has placed in your tongue and shall greet the Son for His honourable company, for He was a preacher himself, and shall thank the Holy Spirit for His grace, because He is master of all gifts. Then the preachers of God, and the holy martyrs, and the loving virgins shall rise up for they are paid the greatest honour in special clothing and in beautiful song and in the wonderful chaplets that they wear to the honour of God. The clothing of the virgins is lily white, the clothing of the preachers is fiery bright as the sun, the clothing of the martyrs is a glistening rosy red, for they suffered a bloody death with Jesus. The virgins' chaplet is of many colours, the crown of the martyrs is strikingly large, the chaplet of the preachers is made entirely of flowers; these are the words of God, which have brought them to great honour here. Thus, this blessed company of three groups dances rejoicing into the presence of the Holy Trinity in a sweet roundelay. Then a threefold, sparkling current flows towards them from God, which fills their spirit so that they sing the truth with joy and without effort, as God has inspired them. This is what the preachers sing: 'O excellent Lord, we have followed your generous goodness in voluntary poverty and have gathered in your stray sheep, which your paid shepherds let stray from the right path.' This is what the martyrs sing: 'Lord, your innocent blood has given our death fulfilment so that we are your companions in martyrdom.'

These blessed, who now hover in Heaven and live there so wonderfully, are bathed in light and are suffused with love and are united in one will, but they do not yet have the honour which resides in the magnificent chairs. They are resting in the might of God and floating in bliss and hold themselves in God's breath as air in the sunlight. But after the Day of Judgement, when God wishes to have supper, then the brides shall be seated opposite their Bridegroom and so love shall come to love, body to the soul and they shall then have full power in eternal honour.

O You lovely Lamb and delightful Young Man, Jesus, Child of the heavenly Father, when You rise up and travel through all the choirs and beckon lovingly to the virgins, then they will follow You, full of praise, into that most overwhelming place, about which I can say no more to anyone. The way in which they shall then play with You and feast on the delight of Your love; that is such intimate sweetness and such intense union that I know of nothing like it.

The widows, too, shall also follow with the longing of their hearts and they are wholly satisfied with the sweet contemplation of the Lamb in union with the virgins. Married people shall also look on this lovingly, at a distance determined by their worth; for the more one is satisfied here with earthly things, the less remains to us there of heavenly bliss.

The choirs all have a special brightness in their radiance, as does Heaven. This radiance is so wondrously magnificent that I neither can nor wish to describe it. God has bestowed so much splendour on the choirs and Heaven that I can convey no more than an inkling of it, no more than the honeybee can carry on its leg from the full honeycomb. In the first choir is bliss, the greatest of all the gifts they have; in the second choir there is gentleness; in the third there is loveliness; in the fourth, sweetness; in the fifth, happiness; in the sixth, noble fragrance; in the seventh, splendour; in the eighth, dignity; in the ninth, ardent love; in the sweet void, pure holiness. The greatest thing about the throne is mighty honour and powerful dominion. The greatest of all that ever was in Heaven is wonder. The greatest thing they can see is what is now and always shall be. Ah, the magnificent space and sweet eternity, and the powerful penetration of all things, and the special intimacy that exists unceasingly between God and each soul that is of such overwhelming tenderness that, even if I had all the wisdom of mankind and all the voices of the angels, I could not express it.

Unbaptised children under the age of five occupy a special place of honour that God has made ready for them from within His Kingdom. They have not grown to the stature of thirty years, because they were not Christians with Christ.[54] They have no crown, there is nothing for God to reward them for; but He has given them of His goodness that they may live in great contentment. The greatest thing they have is the fullness of grace. This is what they sing: 'We praise Him who created us, although we never saw Him; if we had to suffer pain, then we would lament, but we have reason now to be in good spirits.'

Now, some people might wonder at how a sinful person like

---

[54] In the Middle Ages it was thought that all the dead would rise up on the Day of Judgement as thirty-year-olds, because that was the age of Christ upon his resurrection. Cf. Schmidt (1995: 367f., n. 112).

myself has come to write down such things. I tell you in all truth: had God not captured my heart with a special gift seven years ago, I would still be silent and would never have done it. Now I have never suffered harm from God's goodness; this is because of the clear reflection of my sinfulness that is so evident to my soul and because of the nobility of grace that lies in the true gift of God. Indeed, the higher the Soul is raised, the less attention should be paid to the Body in word and deed; there should be no complaint about troubles in its sight, for it is by nature a coward. It should be treated like an old prebendary, who, because he can no longer serve at court, receives alms only through love of God. This is truly useful, for the more noble the dog the tighter the collar![55]

Now dear Lord, I commend this writing to Your generous goodness and beg You, my very dear Love, with a sighing heart and with weeping eyes and with a wretched soul that no Pharisee may ever read it; and I beg You further, dear Lord, that Your children may understand these words in that spirit of very truth in which You communicated them.

III, 3. A lament that the Soul is a handmaid of the love of God

'O Lord, what a wretched and desolate Soul that is, that here on earth is a handmaid of Your love! O, who will help me lament the degree of pain she is in? For she doesn't know herself what it is that she is missing.'

'Lady Bride, in the Book of Love you tell your lover that he should flee from you.[56] You must tell me, Lady, just what came over you; for, if it were possible, I would rather die in pure love, than bid God leave me in darkened wisdom. When I may play with my Love passionately, then wisdom can teach me no discretion. However, when I work at other things with my five senses, then I welcome the holy measure it may bring me.'

'Listen to me, dear companion! I was happily half drunk on love, that is why I speak gently about the senses. However, whenever I am fully drunk, then I can give no thought to my body, for Love has me in her control; her wish is my command, and I am ready to do whatever God hopes for, for if He takes my body, the soul is His. If you want to go to the wine cellar with me, you must pay a high price. If

---

[55] This is a puzzling sentence. It sounds like a proverb or an idiom, but the significance of it is not immediately obvious.

[56] The 'Book of Love' is the Old Testament Song of Songs.

you have a thousand marks that will all be spent in an hour. If you wish to drink unadulterated wine, you will always consume more than you have money for and so the innkeeper will not be able to pour you enough; then you will become poor and naked and scorned by all those who prefer to disport themselves in the mire rather than squander their riches in the grand wine cellar. You will also have to suffer the envy of those who go with you to the wine cellar. Oh, how much they will sometimes scorn you because they do not have the courage to pay so much! They want water mixed with the wine.'

'Dear Lady Bride, I shall willingly drink away all I have in the inn and shall allow myself to be hauled over the coals of love and to be beaten with the firebrands of contempt so that I may frequently go to the blessed wine cellar. I choose this eagerly because I cannot lose in love. And so it is that he, who torments and scorns me, pours me out that wine which the Innkeeper drank himself.[57] I become so drunk on this wine that I become truly subservient to all creatures; it seems to me that, measured against my human baseness and the unworthiness that I am guilty of, no one has ever behaved so badly towards me that he might be guilty of a sin against my accursed self. That is why I cannot avenge myself on my enemies, although I know full well that in their treatment of me they should not break God's commandment either.'

'Dear companion, when it is time to close the wine cellar then, in the street, you must walk hungry, poor, naked and so scorned that you have none of the food of Christian life about you other than faith. If you can still love then, then you will never be ruined.'

'Lady Bride, I have such a hunger for the heavenly Father that I forget all my troubles, and I have such a thirst for His Son that it takes from me all earthly pleasure, and I have such a need for the spirit of both of Them that it transcends the wisdom of the Father, which I cannot grasp, and goes beyond the Son's passion, which I cannot endure, and beyond the consolation of the Holy Spirit, which I cannot embrace.'Whoever is enmeshed in this need must for ever more hang blissfully bound in God.[58]

---

[57] Cf. II, 24 (p. 45) where Mechthild talks of the gall that is poured out for her to drink.

[58] Cf. II, 24 (p. 47) where Mechthild discourses on what she understands by 'bound' and 'unbound' love.

III, 9. Of the beginning of all things, which God has created out of love

Ah, Father of all goodness! I, an unworthy person, thank You for all the love, with which You have drawn me out of myself into Your wonders, so that, Lord, I have heard You in the completeness of Your Trinity and witnessed the high council, which took place before our time, when You, Lord, were enclosed within Yourself alone and your ineffable bliss was shared by no one.[59] Then the Three Persons shone so beautifully in One, that each of them shone through the other and yet were still One. The Father was Himself adorned in the magnificent spirit of omnipotence and the Son resembled the Father in ineffable wisdom and the Holy Spirit both of Them in perfect bounteousness. Then the Holy Spirit played for the Father bounteously and plucked[60] the Holy Trinity and said to Him: 'Lord, dear Father, I want to give you a piece of bountiful advice from out of yourself: we no longer wish to remain sterile in this way. We shall have a created kingdom, and the angels should be made in my likeness, that they are one spirit with me [and man shall be the other]. For, dear Father, that would be pure joy, if they were gathered together in a great host and in ineffable wonder before your eyes.' Then the Father said: 'You are one spirit with me. That which you counsel and desire is pleasing to me.' You know well what took place when the angel was created: Even had the fall of the angels been avoided, man would have had to be created. The Holy Spirit shared His bounteousness with the angels so that they serve us and rejoice in all our good fortune. Then the eternal Son spoke with great deference: 'Dear Father, my nature should also bear fruit; since we wish to bring about wonders then let us create man in my image; although I foresee great sorrow, I must nonetheless love mankind eternally.' Then the Father spoke: 'Son, I too am moved by a powerful desire in my divine breast and I am throbbing with love. We shall become fertile that we may be loved in return and that our great honour might in some measure be recognised. I shall create for myself a bride, who shall greet me with her lips and wound me with her looks and only then shall the loving begin.' Then the Holy Spirit spoke to the Father: 'Yes, dear Father, I shall bring this bride to your bed.' Then the Son spoke: 'Father, you know well that I shall yet die for love; however,

[59] Cf. VI, 31 (p. 115f.).
[60] That is, the harp of the Trinity. On Mechthild's use of the harp as a mystical image, see Schmidt (1995: xxvf.).

let us begin these things joyfully in great holiness.' Then the Holy Trinity turned to the creation of all things and made body and soul for us in ineffable love. Adam and Eve were formed and given a noble nature after the eternal Son, Who is born of the Father without a beginning. Then the Son shared with Adam His heavenly wisdom and His earthly power so that in perfect love he had true understanding and holy senses and was able to command all earthly creatures; we are far removed from that now.

Then God gave Adam in great love a demure, noble, delicate young lady, that was Eve, and graced her with His Son's delightful, splendid demeanour, that the Son Himself bore to honour His Father. Their bodies were to be pure, for God never created shameful parts, and they were clothed in the dress of the angels. They were to conceive their children in holy love, as the sun shines brightly into the water and yet the water is undisturbed.[61] But when they ate the forbidden fruit, then their bodies became shamefully deformed, as is still evident in us today. Had the Holy Trinity created us so ugly, then we could never be ashamed of our being because of its noble nature.

The heavenly Father shared His divine love with the Soul and said: 'I am God of all gods, you are the goddess of all creatures and I give you my pledge of honour that I shall never desert you; if you do not lose yourself, then my angels shall serve you for ever.[62] I shall give you my Holy Spirit as a chamberlain that you might not commit any mortal sin unwittingly, and I give you great freedom of will; my love above all loves, now proceed wisely. You should observe a simple command so that you bear in mind that I am your God.' The very pure food, which God had promised them in Paradise, was to remain in great holiness in their bodies. But when they had eaten the disgusting food, which did not agree with their pure bodies, then they were so full of poison that they lost the purity of the angels and forgot their virginal chastity. Then the soul keened and howled in the darkness for many years for her Love and cried: 'O dear Lord, what has become of Your exquisitely sweet love? How you have called your rightful queen a harlot! This is what the prophets mean.[63] O great Lord, how can You suffer this long torment without ending our death? And yet You do want to be born; but, Lord, all Your deeds are truly perfect, and so Your anger is also.'

[61] Cf. the description of the Virgin Mary's conception of Christ (V, 23 [p. 94f.]).
[62] On the description of the Soul as a goddess see p. 53, n. 53.
[63] In the Old Testament, the prophets often call Israel a harlot for having been unfaithful to God. Cf. Isaiah 1: 21, Jeremiah 3: 6–10 and Ezekiel 16 and 23.

Then another high council was held in the Holy Trinity. Then the eternal Father said: 'I regret my work, for the Bride I had given my Holy Trinity was so pleasing that the highest angels should have been her servants. Indeed, had Lucifer kept his honour, she would have been his goddess, for the bridal bed[64] was intended for her alone; then she no longer wished to be like me. Now she is deformed and of hideous appearance, who would take this dirt to himself?' Ah, then the eternal Son kneeled before His Father and said: 'Dear Father, I shall. If You will give me Your blessing, I will willingly take bloodied mankind upon myself and I shall anoint the wounds of man with the blood of my innocence and shall bandage all the injuries of man with a cloth of wretched ignominy until my end and, dear Father, I shall make amends for the guilt of man by dying a human death.' Then the Holy Spirit spoke to the Father: 'O almighty God, we shall have a fine procession and shall descend separately in great glory from these heights with great honour. I have already been a chamberlain to Mary.' Then the Father, in great love, bowed to the will of both of Them and said to the Holy Spirit: 'You shall carry my light before my Son into all those hearts, which He shall move with words, and, Son, you shall take up your cross. I shall be with you wherever you go and I shall give you a pure virgin for a mother, that you may carry base mankind all the more honourably.' Then the splendid procession descended with great joy into the Temple of Solomon;[65] almighty God wanted to take up residence there for nine months.

III, 14. Of false virtues; he who lives in them lives in lies
I have a master, that is the Holy Spirit, who teaches me very gently what He wants and the rest He keeps from me. Now He speaks thus: 'Wisdom that is not grounded in the Holy Spirit becomes in the end a mountain of arrogance.

Peace without the restraint of the Holy Spirit quickly becomes an empty rage.

Humility without the fire of love becomes in the end open hypocrisy.

Justice without the depth of God's humility quickly turns into dreadful hatred.

Poverty with constant greed is in itself a sinful excess.

Dreadful fear with true guilt brings horrifying impatience.

---

[64] Cf. p. 30, n. 7.
[65] A mystical image for the Virgin Mary.

Fine behaviour with wolfish intent quickly becomes apparent to the wise.

Holy longing from complete integrity comes to no one without effort.

A comfortable life without adversity is slow to engage in useful things.

Presumptuous virtue without God's grace is felled by pride.

Fine promises without faithful deeds is falsehood counselled by the devil.

Kind consolation without the true surety of the soul and of the Holy Spirit leads in the end to an unhappy death.

Great patience without inclining one's heart towards God is a secret guilt, for all those who do not depend on the truth of God in all things shall fall away from the eternal God in great shame.

Love without humility for a mother and holy fear for a father is orphaned of all virtues.'

III, 15. You should approach God's table with eight virtues. With the pledge of redemption a person redeemed seventy thousand souls from the dreadful and manifold fires of Purgatory

O you very foolish beguines, how shameless you are that you do not tremble in the presence of our Almighty Judge since you so often take communion out of blind habit! Now I, who am the least amongst you, must feel shame, sweat and tremble.[66]

One feast day I was so overwhelmed that I did not dare receive Him,[67] for in His presence I was ashamed of my greatest virtue. Then I asked my very dear Love if He might show me His glory on this occasion. Then He said: 'Truly, if you go before me in humble sorrow and in holy fear, then I have to follow you as the high flood water does the deep mill stream. But, if you approach me with the blooming desire of flowing love,[68] then I must meet you and caress you with my divine nature as my only queen.' 'I have to speak in my own right if I am to be truly capable of fully expressing God's goodness. I was no more held back by that than a hot oven would be in baking a load of white rolls.' Then I went to God's table in noble company; they were devoted in their care of me but also kept a sharp

---

[66] This is the only occasion on which Mechthild identifies herself explicitly as a beguine.

[67] That is, the host.

[68] Cf. p. 28, n. 5.

eye on me. Truth reproached me, Fear scolded me, Shame scourged me, Remorse condemned me, Desire drew me, Love led me, Christian Faith protected me, Faithful Intention in all good things prepared me and all my Good Deeds wailed over me, mighty God received me, His pure humanity merged with mine, his Holy Spirit comforted me. Then I said: 'Lord, now You are mine, for You have been given to me today and also in that passage where it is said: *Puer natus est nobis*.[69] Now I desire, Lord, Your praise and not my advantage, so that today Your noble body might come as comfort to poor souls. You are truly mine; now You should, Lord, be a pledge of redemption today for those who are held captive.'

Then the Soul acquired such power that she led Him with His strength and they came to a place that was as dreadful as human eye ever lit upon; an awful bath had been made ready, a mixture of fire and of pitch, of filth, smoke and stench. A dense, dark pall was spread over it like a black skin. The souls lay there in it like toads in the mire. They looked human in form, but they were spirits and had the devil's likeness about them. They stewed and roasted together. They screamed and suffered inexpressible torment because of their flesh that had brought them so low. Their flesh had blinded their spirit, it was because of this that they stewed most. Then the human Spirit spoke: 'O Lord, how many are there of these poor people? You are my true pledge, You must now show mercy.' Then Our Lord said: 'There are more than can be counted, and you cannot comprehend the number as long as your flesh shall have an earthly share in you. They were all broken vessels and neglected their spiritual life on earth. They are from all stations in life and from all lands.' Then the human Spirit asked: 'Ah dear Lord, where are the hermits, I don't see any of them here?' Then Our Lord answered: 'Their sins were clandestine, now they are bound to the devils, alone in this abyss.' Then the human Soul was greatly distressed and prostrated herself at the feet of Our dear Lord and pleaded mightily and laboured lovingly and said: 'Dear Love, You know well what I want.' Then Our Lord said: 'It is right that you have brought me here, I shall not be unmindful of them.' Then there was around her a very great throng of devils who were busying themselves with those in the unholy bath – they were also beyond counting – rubbing them, washing them and eating them and satisfying themselves and they whipped them with

---

[69] 'For unto us a child (boy) is born' (Isaiah 9: 6). This is from the introit of the third mass of the Feast of the Nativity of the Lord.

fiery scourges. Then the human Spirit said this to them: 'Listen, you gluttons of sin, look at this pledge! Is it not precious enough to satisfy you?' Then they were frightened, quaking in awful shame and said: 'Yes, now take them away from here. However godless we might be, we have to speak the truth to you.' Then Our Lord granted the poor souls a sweet wish from His divine heart. Then they got out in great joy and love. Then the stranger Soul said: 'Ah dear Lord, where should they go now?' Then He said: 'I shall bring them to a mountain covered with flowers; there they will find more bliss than I can tell of.' Then Our Lord waited on them and was their chamberlain and their very dear companion. Then Our Lord said to me that there were seventy thousand of them there. Then the Soul asked in return how long their suffering should have been. Then Our Lord said: 'They have been separated from their bodies for thirty years and they would have been in torment for another ten years had not such a noble pledge been given for them.' The devils fled from them and did not dare to take it. 'Dear Love,' said the Soul again, 'how long shall they be here?' Then Our Lord answered and said: 'As long as seems right to us.'

III, 20. Of five prophets who illumine this book
Our Lord has promised me He would illumine this book with five lights:

Moses' great intimacy[70] and his holy work and the particular humiliation which he endured through no fault of his own, and the wonderful signs granted to him and his sweet teaching and the privileged dialogue of love which he frequently entered into with eternal God on the high mountain – all this shall be a light, and God has given and will continue to give me this so that in His protection I may walk, free of guilty shame, through all the evil snares of my enemies and be upheld in love, just as Moses was with his friends when they went through the Red Sea; and Pharaoh and his friends shall not chase us too far. Alas, how they drowned in this sea! Ah, be merciful, dear Lord, so that our enemies will be converted.

King David is the second light in this book with his Psalter, in which he teaches and laments, beseeches, exhorts and praises God.

The words of Solomon illumine – but not his deeds, for he himself is darkened – in the Song of Songs where the Bride is so boldly drunk

---

[70] That is, with God.

and the Bridegroom speaks to her so ardently: 'You are so beautiful, my love, and without blemish.'[71]

Jeremiah also illumines for his part when he speaks of the mystery of Our Lady; for God has told me that he possessed pure chastity and sublime love and that he suffered torment in Christian faith, which he never witnessed with the eyes of his body.[72]

Daniel also illumines in a wonderful way, for God in His grace gave him food for both body and soul in the midst of all his enemies.[73] The same thing has happened to my unworthy self in times of need; my enemies have seen a little of this and cannot bear it; that is why they make me suffer.

III, 21. Of Hell; how it has three parts; how Lucifer and sixteen kinds of people are tormented; there is no help for them. Of Lucifer's clothing

I have seen a place, its name is everlasting enmity; it is built in the deepest abyss with the stones of various mortal sins.[74] Pride was the first stone, as was clearly evident in Lucifer. Disobedience, base greed, gluttony, lust, these were four heavy stones, which our father Adam was the first to send there. Anger, falseness and murder, these three stones were brought there by Cain. Lying, betrayal, despair of God and suicide, with these four stones wretched Judas also took his own life. The sins of Sodom and hypocritical holiness, these are the dreadful cornerstones which are built into the structure.

This place has been under construction for many years; woe to all those who have lent a helping hand. The more they send in advance, the more they will be received with great ignominy if they follow themselves.

This place is so perverted that the most high-ranking are allocated the lowest and most ignoble position. Lucifer sits in the deepest abyss, bound by his guilt, and out of his fiery heart and out of his mouth there is a constant stream of all the sins, torments, sickness

---

71 Cf. Song of Songs 4: 7.

72 Cf. Jeremiah 31: 22. This passage was interpreted in patristic theology as a prophecy of the Incarnation.

73 Cf. Daniel 14: 30.

74 In moral theology, a distinction is made between mortal and venial sins. Mortal sin is the most serious category of sin. According to Catholic teaching, such sin consists of a deliberate act of turning away from God, of frustrating his purpose. This sin incurs the loss of sanctifying grace and eternal damnation, unless it is followed by adequate repentance.

and disgrace in which Hell, Purgatory and Earth are so wretchedly caught up. In the deepest part of Hell the fire and the darkness and stench and terror and all kinds of pain are greatest, and it is here that Christians are ranged according to their deeds. In the middle part of Hell the various torments are more moderate, the Jews are ranged here according to their deeds. In the uppermost part of Hell the various torments are the least intense, and there the heathens are ranged according to their deeds. This is how the heathens lament: 'Alas, if only we had had a law, then we would not be in such pain eternally.' The Jews also lament, saying: 'Alas, if only we had followed God in the teaching of Moses, then we would not have been so greatly damned.' The Christians lament even more, that through self-will they have forfeited that great honour, when Christ in great love had chosen them to be His own; in great distress, they look upon Lucifer all the time and, naked, they must publicly parade before him with all their guilt. Alas, with what ignominy they are received by him! He greets them horribly and speaks bitterly: 'You who are damned with me, what joy do you seek here? You have certainly never heard good said of me, so how could you feel comfortable now?'

Then he takes hold of the proud man first of all and thrusts him under his tail and says this: 'I have not sunk so low that I cannot still lord it over you.' All the sodomites pass down through his throat and live in his belly; when he draws breath they are pulled into his belly, but when he coughs they are pushed out again. The hypocrites he takes on his lap and he kisses them in a very ghastly way and says: 'You are my companions. I was also clothed in beautiful falseness, you have all been betrayed by that.' He gnaws at the money-lender incessantly and reminds him that he was never merciful. The robber he robs himself and then hands him over to his fellows that they might hunt him and beat him and have no mercy on him. The thief hangs by his feet and is a vessel of light in Hell; and yet the accursed see no better for it. Those who have been unchaste together must here lie bound together before Lucifer; but if one of them arrives there alone, then the devil is his mate. The disbelieving masters sit at Lucifer's feet so that they must look directly at their unclean god. He conducts a disputation with them so that they might be disgraced. The avaricious man Lucifer devours, because he always wanted to have more. After he has swallowed him he excretes him from under his tail. The murderers must stand, covered in blood, before him and must be dealt fiery blows of the sword by the devil. Those who have acted here out of dreadful hatred must there be his smelling-bottle and always hang under his nose. Those who here applied themselves so vigorously to drinking and eating in excess must stand everlastingly hungry before Lucifer and eat burning stones and drink sulphur and pitch. There all sweetness is exchanged for sourness; we see how we conduct ourselves here. The slothful man is burdened there with all torments, the irascible man is beaten there with fiery whips. The very wretched minstrel, who through an exaltation of spirits[75] can excite to sinful vanity, weeps more tears in Hell than there is water in the sea.

Underneath Lucifer I saw the bedrock of Hell, that is, a hard, black flint-stone; it shall support the structure for evermore. Although there is neither bottom nor boundary to Hell, it has in its ordering both depth and finiteness. How Hell roars and rages in itself and how the devils fight with the souls, and how they stew and roast, and how they swim and wade in the stench and morass and among the serpents and in the mire, and how they bathe in sulphur and pitch, that can never be fully described either by themselves or anyone else.

After I had seen this distress, through no effort on my part but by the grace of God, then I, poor wretch, was so afflicted by the stench and the unearthly heat that I could neither sit nor walk and was bereft of my five senses for three days, like someone who has been hit by a thunderbolt. My soul, however, suffered no harm, for she had not been brought there by the sickness that is called everlasting death. But if it were possible that a pure soul could be with them, that would be an eternal light and a great consolation to them; for it is in the nature of the innocent Soul that she must always illumine and shine, because she has been born of the eternal light painlessly. However, if she assumes the devil's likeness then she loses her beautiful light. Can the damned in everlasting Hell receive some consolation from prayers and alms? I have not heard of that. Because they are always in such a dreadful state of mind they shudder at the sight of anything good.

After the Day of Judgement Lucifer shall put on a new garment that is the product of the muck of all the filthy sins that he was ever able to make known to mankind or the angels, for he is the prime vessel of all sins. Thus he is then unleashed and yet his fury and his dreadfulness are so infused in all souls and in all devils that his presence is always felt. Then he shall on occasion inflate himself to such

---

[75] '[M]it hohem muote' – this phrase is often used in courtly poetry to describe the state of exhilaration experienced by the lover when his lady pays him attention.

an extent and his jaws open so wide that he shall swallow in one intake of breath Christians, Jews and heathens. Then they shall reap their full reward in his belly and have their special feast. O woe then body and soul! What the human mouth can tell of this is nothing compared to the immeasurable distress that is suffered there. For truly, I cannot bear to think of this any longer than it takes to say Hail Mary. Alas, it is so dreadful there.

At its top Hell has a head that is so monstrous and has so many horrible eyes, from which flames shoot out and engulf the poor souls who live in the gatehouse from where God had taken Adam and others of our forefathers. Now that is the greatest Purgatory to which a sinner can come. I saw there bishops, governors and great lords in prolonged distress through inexpressible suffering. All those who arrive there have only just been spared everlasting Hell by God, for I found no one at all there who at their death had made a pure confession through the mouth of their body. When their physical senses were taken from them at death, the Body lay still, and yet Soul and Body both had one will; when they had lost the darkness of Earth then God gave them true knowledge in secret. Oh, how narrow is the path to the Kingdom of Heaven! Then together as one, the Body and Soul, who were not yet separated, spoke thus: 'True God, have mercy, I am truly sorry for my sins.' This is a short space of time in which God has secretly regained many an apparently lost soul. I have found that this only happens to someone who has done something good out of good will. The devils lead the sullied souls from the body to Purgatory, for the pure angels may not touch them because they do not have the same radiance. However, a soul may have the help of friends on Earth, so that the devils are prevented from constantly attacking the soul. If she is very guilty, she must suffer other torments; she can put up with that much better than if the devils should catch her and have her for their sport.

What our holy forefathers took with them when they went to Hell was sincere hope in Christian faith with holy love of God and a great number of humble virtues and faithful effort. Although they went to Hell, they were ready for the Kingdom of Heaven. Nothing in Hell could harm them. It was the love that they brought with them that protected them from burning. This must burn eternally in the children of God, otherwise they will never get to Heaven. God has ordained the following: Whatever we take with us from here, we must eat and drink there. But the negligent, who depart from here without having done penance for great sins, cannot experience anything worse, short of being damned, than being in front of the mouth of Hell, where at all times Lucifer's breath strikes out with every torment and courses through them so excruciatingly that these poor wretches are as united in the flames and in the manifold horror as their very blessed forefathers were united in the sweet familiar love of God. I saw no women there other than high-ranking princesses, who here on earth indulge in all sorts of sins together with the princes.

Up at the top of Hell there is a mouth, which is open at all times. All those who enter this mouth will never be delivered from everlasting death.

Book IV

At the outset of this book, Mechthild provides an account (IV, 2) of what motivated her to take up the religious life. She couches this account of her spiritual life in terms of the tradition of *sancta simplicitas* ['holy simplicity']. Her writing is presented as an act of religious obedience as she makes clear the divine nature of her impulse to write and the authority she receives from God, as well as the sanction and encouragement given her by her confessor. Mechthild states programmatically that the purpose of her book is to glorify God and to instruct her contemporaries. In the course of her writings Mechthild imparts much phenomenological information about her mystical and visionary experiences. This is expressed quintessentially in IV, 13 where she insists on the apprehension of her spiritual rather than her physical senses.

In this book there is a concentration of chapters (IV, 20; IV, 21; IV, 22) which have as their focus the praise of St Dominic and the Order of Preachers. The tension that existed between the clergy and the mendicant orders over the matter of priestly office and the administering of the sacraments is reflected in Mechthild's writings. She supports the right of the Dominicans to preach, hear confession and conduct Mass wherever they choose. In the first of three apocalyptic visions (IV, 27) Mechthild reveals how, at the end of time, the Order of Preachers will be surpassed by another order.

In IV, 12 Mechthild, in her role as a bride of the Trinity, opens up another, highly distinctive aspect of her union with God. Here mystical union through erotic encounter is supplanted by estrangement from the Bridegroom. In imitation of the kenotic Christ who suffers and dies on the cross,[76] she 'flows down' and 'sinks' from ecstasy into pain, humility and finally estrangement from God. Paradoxically, it is in this estrangement that she finds her most intimate form of union.

---

[76] Kenosis is the concept of the condescension and the self-limitation of the Logos in incarnation. On Mechthild's identity with the kenotic Christ, see McGinn (1998: 241ff.).

The concluding chapter (IV, 28) has been interpreted as the conclusion to an early version of Mechthild's book.

IV, 2. This book has come from God; the Soul praises herself in a number of ways; she is given two angels and two wicked devils. She does battle against the flesh with twelve virtues

All the days of my life before I began this book and before a single word had entered my soul from God, I was one of the most innocent people who ever took up the religious life. I knew nothing of the devil's wickedness, I had no experience of the frailty of the world, I was also unaware of the falseness of religious people. I must speak to glorify God and also because of the teaching in this book. Unworthy sinner that I am, in my twelfth year I was greeted, while alone, by such an outflowing from the Holy Spirit that after that I could never find it in myself to commit any grave venial sin.[77] This very precious greeting came every day and lovingly turned all the sweetness of the world to sorrow for me and the strength of this greeting is still growing day for day. This happened for thirty-one years. I knew no more of God other than through Christian faith, and I always made great efforts to keep my heart pure. God Himself is my witness that I never, either through will or desire, asked Him to give me these things which are written in this book. Neither did I ever imagine that this could happen to people. While I was with my family and other friends, to whom I was always most dear, I knew nothing of these things. Now I had for a long time longed to be held in contempt through no fault of my own. So, out of love for God, I went to a place where I had no friends save one. I was worried that, because of this person, holy contempt and the pure love of God would be withheld from me. However, God never deserted me and transported me into such lovely sweetness, into such holy knowledge and into such incomprehensible wonders that I had little use for earthly things.

Then, for the first time, my spirit was transported out of my prayers to between Heaven and air; then I saw with the eyes of my soul in heavenly bliss the beautiful humanity of Our Lord Jesus Christ, and I recognised in His noble countenance the Holy Trinity, the eternity of the Father, the passion of the Son, the sweetness of the

---

[77] A venial sin, unlike a mortal sin, is pardonable and merits a temporal rather than an eternal penalty. It may be remitted in confession, but it can also be expiated in other ways, for example by fasting, almsgiving and especially by prayer.

Holy Spirit. Then I saw the angel, into whose care I was given at baptism, and my devil. Then Our Lord said: 'I shall take this angel from you and will give you two in return; they shall look after you in these wonders.' When the Soul looked at the two angels, oh how startled she was in humble helplessness and she prostrated herself at the feet of Our Lord and thanked Him and bewailed her unworthiness at having such princes as her chamberlains. One of the angels was from the Seraphim and he burns in love and is a holy light for the favoured Soul. The other angel was from the Cherubim; he guards the gifts of grace and orders wisdom in the loving Soul.

Then Our Lord bid two devils come forward; they were great masters and had been taken from Lucifer's school, from where they seldom emerged. When the Soul looked at the very horrible devils, then she shuddered a little and entrusted herself to Our Lord and yet accepted them willingly. One of the devils is a deceiver, dressed in the beautiful robes of an angel. O, how many cunning, false snares he laid before me at first! Once during Mass he came from on high and said: 'Now, I am very beautiful. Would you not like to worship me?' Then the Soul answered: 'We should worship God alone in times of good fortune and in times of need.' Then he said: 'Will you not look up and see who I am.' Then he displayed beneath the air a beautiful false radiance that has led many a heretic astray, and said: 'You alone shall be the most exalted virgin on the seat of the throne and I the most handsome young man beside you.' Then she replied: 'It would be foolish to take the worst when the best is within reach.' Then he said: 'Since you will not give yourself to me and you are so holy and I so humble, then I will worship you.' Then she said: 'You will receive no grace from worshipping a quagmire.' Then he showed her the five wounds painted on his hands and feet and said: 'Now you see truly who I am; if you will live according to my counsel, I will give you great honour. You should tell people about this grace, for much good would come of it.' Although his useless talk irritated her greatly, she listened to it willingly so that she might learn from it, and then she said: 'You tell me you are God; now tell me who this might be who, as the host here in the hands of the true priest, is the Son of the living God.' At that he wanted to leave and she said: 'By almighty God, I now warn you to listen to me: I know what your game is; if I were to tell everyone the secret of my heart, the pleasure I would have would be short-lived, for you would be intent on wrecking that enjoyment. You would do this so that I might fall into despair and sadness and into unbelief and incontinence and after that into everlasting heartache; and you also do this so that I should think that you come to me like this because I am so holy. Well, you ancient trickster, as long as God stands by me all your effort is in vain.' Then he shouted 'A curse on your sorcery, let me go now, I will never trouble you again.'

The other devil that was given to me is a troublemaker and a master of hidden incontinence. God had forbidden him, however, ever to come to me himself. But he sends perverted people to me as messengers, who distort my good deeds and with their words detract from my honour whatever they can. He is also intent on the following: that when good people are together, they talk idly in an incontinent way; this cannot but distress me. I had never experienced this before.

One night I was saying my prayers before first sleep. Then this same devil flew through the air and observed this sinful Earth very closely. He was as big as a giant, he had a short tail and a crooked nose, his head was as big as a washtub, fiery sparks in black flames flew out of his mouth. Then he laughed with cunning force and a very dreadful voice. Then the Soul asked him why he was laughing, what he was looking for and what he was doing. Then he answered and said: 'Since I cannot torment you myself, I am indeed pleased that I find so many who appear to be angels and are happy to torment you for me.' Then he went on: 'I am the chamberlain of religious people and I look for two kinds of weakness in them that separate them from God most quickly: that is concealed or secret incontinence. Wherever a person in the religious life seeks without real need the pleasure of their flesh in all the five senses then they become incontinent, that is coarse and sluggish and the true love of God grows cold. The second weakness is hidden hatred in open discord. This is a useful sin to me; wherever I find that it has been slept on unrepented, that is my gain, for this is a foundation for protracted malice and a loss of all holiness.' Then the Soul said: 'Now, by nature you have nothing good about you; how can it be that you lay before me this useful information about your wickedness?' Then he replied: 'Wherever I go, God has me so firmly in His hands that I can do nothing other than what He directs me to.'

Wretched person that I am, I was guilty of such great sin in my early childhood that, had I not repented and confessed, I would have had to spend ten years in Purgatory. Now, dear Lord, when I die I will happily suffer there for love of you. It is not reason that urges me to say this, but love. When I took up the religious life and took leave of the world, then I looked at my body; it was well armed against my poor soul with mighty strength in abundance and with all the power of nature. Then I realised that it was my enemy, and also realised that if I were to escape everlasting death, then I would have to defeat it and so a battle had to be begun. And so then I considered the weapons of my soul, the noble martyrdom of Our Lord Jesus Christ; with that I armed myself. Then I had to be constantly in great fear and throughout my youth had to strike my body with heavy defensive blows: these were sighing, weeping, confessing, fasting, keeping vigil, flagellation and constant worship. These were the weapons of my soul with which I overcame my body so greatly that, in twenty years, there was never a time that I was not tired, sick and weak, first of all from repentance and suffering, after that from holy desire and from spiritual effort and, in addition, from many heavy days of physical sickness. Furthermore, mighty Love came upon me and taxed me so with these wonders that I could not remain silent about them; but I was then greatly troubled by my ignorance. Then I said: 'Ah bounteous God, what have You seen in me? You know very well that I am a fool, a sinful and a wretched person in body and soul. You should have given these things to learned people for that would have brought You praise.' Then Our Lord was very angry with the poor wretch that I am and asked me for my opinion: 'Now tell me, are you mine?' 'Yes, Lord, that is what I desire.' 'May I not then do with you what I want?' 'Yes, most dearly Beloved, please do, even if I should become nothing.' Then Our Lord spoke again: 'You shall follow me in these things and trust me and you shall also be sick for a long time, and I will look after you myself; and all that you need for body and soul I shall provide for you.'

Then I, poor wretch, went to my father confessor, trembling in humble shame and told him all this and begged also for his guidance. Then he said that I should proceed joyfully; God, who had drawn me to Him, would look after me well. Then he instructed me to do what often gives me cause to weep for shame, for I am acutely aware of my own unworthiness; that is, he ordered a pitiful woman to write this book out of the heart and mouth of God. Thus, this book has come lovingly from God and is not drawn from human senses.

IV, 12. How the Bride, who is united with God, rejects the consolation of all creatures, accepting only that of God, and how she sinks in suffering

This is what the Bride of God, who has rested in the locked treasure chamber of the complete Holy Trinity, says: 'Ah, get up and go away from me, all you creatures! You're hurting me and you can't console me.' The creatures ask: 'Why?' The Bride says: 'My love has slipped away from me while I slept, resting in union with Him.'[78] 'Can't this beautiful world and everything that is good in it console you?' 'No, I see the serpent of falsehood and the snares of false cunning in all the sensuous pleasure of this world. I also see the hook of greed in the carrion of base sweetness, with which many are caught.' 'Can Heaven comfort you at all?' 'No, there would only be death there, if it weren't for the living God.' 'Well, Lady Bride, can the saints not console you?' 'No, were they to be separated from the living Godhead that flows through them, they would weep even more than I, for they have risen higher than I have and live deeper in God.' 'Can the Son of God console you at all?' 'Yes, indeed I ask Him when we might walk amongst the flowers of holy knowledge, and I beg Him eagerly to open to me the gates of that sparkling flood which is held in the Holy Trinity and from which alone the Soul lives. If I am to be consoled according to my nobility, then God's breath should draw me in without effort, for the sparkling sun of the living Godhead shines through the clear water of joyful mankind and the sweet pleasure of the Holy Spirit, which has emerged from both of them, has deprived me of all that exists below the Godhead.[79] I have no taste for anything but God, I am wondrously dead. I am most ready to forego this taste willingly that He might be praised wondrously; for when I, an unworthy person, am unable to praise God with my own strength, then I send all creatures to court and bid them praise God for me with all their wisdom, with all their love, with all their beauty and with all their desire, as they were created without sin by God, and with all their voice too, as they now are singing. When I contemplate this great praise, I have no pain anywhere. Nor can I tolerate the touch of any consolation other than that of my Love. I love my earthly friends in heavenly fellowship and I love my enemies in a holy lament for their salvation. God has sufficiency in all things, except in the caressing of the Soul of which He can never have enough.'

After this wonder and this consolation had been going on for eight years, God wanted to console me beyond what my soul deserved. 'Ah no, dear Lord, don't raise me too high', said the unworthy Soul, 'the lowest part is too good for me, I will gladly stay there for the sake of Your honour.' Then the poor thing fell down among those souls that

---

78   This is an allusion to the Song of Songs (Cant.) 3: 1 ('By night on my bed I sought him whom my soul loves: I sought him, but I found him not').

79   In this context the 'nobility' of the Soul is a reference to her origins in God. Cf. I, 22 (pp. 30ff.); I, 44 (p. 35f.); III, 9 (pp. 58ff.); VI, 3 (p. 109).

were waiting and those souls that were damned and this seemed to her too good. Then Our Lord followed her in the way that is bearable to those who are in the lowest place of joy, for God shines in everyone according to the degree they are sanctified here in love and ennobled in virtue. St John says: 'We shall see God as He is.'[80] This is true. But the sun shines according to the weather. Just as there are many kinds of weather under the sun on earth, so there are many dwelling places in the Kingdom of Heaven;[81] furthermore He comes to me in the measure in which I can cope with Him and see Him. Then Our Lord said: 'How long do you want to stay here?' The Bride said: 'Ah, leave me, dear Lord, and let me sink further for the sake of Your honour.' Thereupon both the Soul and the Body came into such a great darkness that I lost my cognitive senses and the light, and I knew nothing of God's intimacy, and most blessed Love also went her way. Then the Soul spoke: 'Where are you now, Lady Fidelity? I shall now entrust to you Love's office and you shall preserve God's honour in me.' Then this lady-in-waiting took her mistress into her care with such holy patience and such cheerful forbearance that I lived untroubled. Then Unbelief came and overwhelmed me with such great darkness and shouted at me in such great rage that the sound of its voice terrified me and it said: 'If this grace had come from God, He would not have abandoned you so.' Then the Soul said: 'Where are you now, Lady Constancy? Tell true Belief to come to me!' Then the Father of the Kingdom of Heaven spoke to the Soul: 'Remember what you have experienced and seen, when there was nothing between you and me.' Then the Son spoke: 'Remember what your body has suffered of my pain.' This is what the Holy Spirit said: 'Remember what you have written.' Then both Soul and Body answered with the constancy of true faith: 'As I have praised, loved and enjoyed and known, so I shall depart from here unchanged.'

After that constant Estrangement from God arrived and so completely enveloped the Soul that the blessed Soul said: 'Welcome, most blessed Estrangement, fortunate am I that I was born, now that you, Lady, shall be my lady-in-waiting; for you bring me unaccustomed joy and incomprehensible wonders and unbearable sweetness as well. But, Lord, you should take this sweetness from me and let me be estranged from you. Ah how fortunate I am, dear God, that I

---

[80] Cf. 1 John 3: 2.
[81] Cf. John 14: 2.

may bear this as is fitting in the vicissitudes of love; for how welcome it is I dare not say, other than that the gall has turned to honey on the palate of my soul.' And then I wanted all creatures to praise Our Lord with *Te deum laudamus*.[82] They did not want to do this and turned their backs on me. Then the Soul's joy knew no bounds and she herself said: 'Look, that you scorn me and turn your back on me, this is my good fortune, this glorifies Our Lord immeasurably. Now His honour is seen in me, for God is now with me in a wondrous way, now that His estrangement is more welcome to me than He Himself is.' The Soul knew this full well when God wanted to console her at the height of the estrangement. Then she said: 'Remember, Lord, who I am and keep your distance from me.' Then Our Lord said to her: 'Allow me to cool the heat of my Godhead, the desire of my Humanity and the pleasure of my Holy Spirit in you.' To this she answered: 'Yes, Lord, but in such a way that it is You, Lord, and not me who benefits.'

After that the Bride came into such darkness that her body sweated and was cramped in pain. Then a person bid her[83] be a messenger for them to God. Then this person said: 'Lady Pain, I ask you now to release me, for at the moment you are the greatest thing about me.' Then Pain rose up out of the Soul and out of the Body like a dark nimbus and went to God with wise intent and shouted in a loud voice: 'Lord, you know well what I want.' Then Our Lord met her before the gate to the Kingdom and said: 'Welcome, Lady Pain, you are the garment that I wore closest to my body on Earth and all the scorn of the world was my best attire. However much I might have loved you there, you shall not enter here; but to the virgin, who wants to do two things, I shall give two things. She shall always be refined and discerning[84] and thus she will help you to be her messenger and then she shall have my embrace and union with my heart.' Then Pain spoke thus: 'Lord, through me many are blessed and yet I myself am not blessed, and I consume many holy bodies and yet I myself am wicked, and I bring many to the Kingdom of

---

82 'We praise you, God.'

83 The 'person' is Mechthild and 'her' is personified Pain. It is a trait of Mechthild's style that she may switch narrative perspective within the course of a chapter. Thus, from talking here about the 'Bride' she suddenly distances the reader from the figure, referring to herself simply as 'a person'. Cf. II, 4 (p. 41); IV, 12 (pp. 73ff.); IV, 22 (p. 78f.); V, 32 (p. 99); VI, 15 (pp. 110ff.); VII, 3 (pp. 123ff.); VII, 8 (p. 125f.). On this aspect of Mechthild's style, see Kasten (1995).

84 Cf. I, 4 (p. 29).

Heaven and yet I never enter there myself.' To this Our Lord answered thus: 'Pain, you were not born of the Kingdom of Heaven and that is why you may not enter there; rather, you were born out of Lucifer's heart, you shall return there and live with him everlastingly.'

'Ah, blessed Estrangement from God, how lovingly I am bound to you! You strengthen my will in pain and make dear to me the long and difficult wait in this poor body. Whatever I do to make you more my companion, the more greatly and marvellously God descends upon me. O Lord, I can not sink away from You in the depths of pure humility; alas, in pride I may easily slip away from You! But the deeper I sink, the sweeter I drink.'

IV, 13. The writing in this book is seen, heard and felt in all the members of the body
I cannot, nor will not, write, unless I see with the eyes of my soul and hear with the ears of my eternal spirit and feel the power of the Holy Spirit in all the members of my body.

IV, 20. Of six virtues of St Dominic
On the feast day of St Dominic I prayed to Our Lord for the community of the Preaching Order. Then it pleased Our dear Lord to come to me Himself and He brought with Him St Dominic, whom, if I may say so, I love above all other saints. Then Our Lord said: 'My son, Dominic, observed four things on earth, which all priors should observe. He loved his brothers so dearly that he could not bear to distress them with things that stemmed from his own wilfulness. The second was that he often improved his food out of love for his brothers and as a help to them, so that young brothers might not think back on the world and old ones might not fall by the way. The third thing, in which, with holy wisdom, he set them an example, was that, for the sake of God, they should be moderate in all their being and in all their habits and in all their needs. The fourth was that he was so compassionate that he never wanted to burden his dear brothers with any penance beyond what the Order laid down for transgression.' Our Lord continued: 'I'll tell you two other things: whenever Dominic laughed, then he laughed with the true sweetness of the Holy Spirit. But when he wept, then he wept with such great loyalty that in his wishes it was always all his brothers whom he brought first to my attention and in addition to them, with all his might, holy Christianity.' Before this I had not known that laughter devoid of foolishness is not sinful.

IV, 21. There are sixteen things that God loves about the Order of Preachers

After this Our dear Lord said: 'There are two things about the Order of Preachers that I love so much that my divine heart smiles continually on them. The one is the holiness of their life, the other is their great benefit to holy Christianity. Furthermore, they greet my Holy Trinity with seven things; these are: powerful sighing, heartfelt weeping, fervent desire, strict discipline, arduous solitariness, faithful humility, joyful love.' Our Lord continued: 'They also honour my three names through the performance of seven things: in songs of praise, through true preaching, right absolution, loving comfort, friendly help, holy example; and they are also a beneficial band of holy Christian faith.' Our beloved Lord carried on: 'The alms, which they give to the needy for love of me, are so holy that the sins of the needy who receive them are diminished and, furthermore, the devil can find no resting place where these alms are eaten. This is because of the holiness of their pleasing poverty.'

Ah, eternal spring of the Godhead, out of which I and all things have flowed, I, unworthy creature, praise you with all that is below you, that I too, Lord, am thus comforted by You. Amen.

IV, 22. Of the fourfold crown of Brother Heinrich and the honour of St Dominic

One holy Easter Sunday a brother of the Order of Preachers died after he had preached, sung Mass and had given people the holy body of Our Lord; and when he had performed all his duties, he asked for extreme unction and passed away towards nightfall. After he had been buried, a person[85] went to his grave and greeted both soul and body; she was in the habit of doing this after the death of religious people; and then God staged a divine celebration in her soul and thus his soul was shown to her as it was held in God's embrace in great honour. Then she saw clearly that his honour was not yet complete, and she asked Our Lord how long he would have to be like this and whether he had suffered anything of Purgatory. Then Our Lord said: 'He shall be like this for a week.' That was seven days and seven nights. He had rested himself in inexpressible delight on God's breast, in the spiritual fervour that he had not been able to enjoy here, and he arrived there so swiftly and painlessly, just as a dear child

---

[85] Cf. p. 76, n. 83.

might be lifted by its mother out of the ashes onto her lap. Then he said: 'Tell my sister I shall console her with God within a fortnight.'

This happened; she died fourteen nights later. Then he invited me to his celebration, at which he was to receive his honour. All the heavenly host made ready for this and gathered together in a magnificent procession. St Dominic came with a great following; they were all preachers, who had died in the Order, and they wore golden crowns, whose value reflected the degree of their holiness in the Order. St Dominic presented a shining crown to Brother Heinrich, which sparkled in its radiance as beautifully as the sun at its most brilliant; he gave this to Heinrich as a reward from God for having followed his holy example in the Order of Preachers.

St Dominic stands out from all the others in unutterable beauty, for he receives special merit from each brother as a reward. I saw him clothed specially in three kinds of honour. He wears a white garment of innate chastity; in addition to that, a green garment of growing knowledge of God; and in addition to that, a red garment held together with clasps, for he suffered spiritual martyrdom. These brothers have a flag in honour of the Order; no one else carries such a thing: a magnificent banner precedes them; they are followed by all those who here adhere to their teaching.

Our Lord sat in His omnipotence and crowned this brother with three kinds of honour; these were: simple obedience, voluntary poverty, constant self-abasement. Then Brother Heinrich thanked Our Lord thus: 'I thank You Lord for finding me, for sustaining me and for accepting me.' Then he bowed to Our Lord and turned to his brothers. Then St Dominic said: 'Welcome, dear son, now enter into the glory of your Lord, alleluia!'

That I should be thus graced and should see this was due in particular to my being estranged for the sake of God and my being constantly and maliciously scorned by friends of God.

IV, 27. Of the end of the Order of Preachers and of the Antichrist, of Enoch and Elijah[86]

The Order of Preachers had come under heavy fire from false masters and from many greedy sinners too.[87] Then I begged Our Dear Lord to protect His own honour in them. Then God said: 'For as

---

[86] Cf. VI, 15; VII, 57.
[87] This is an allusion to the attacks made in the 1250s by William of St Amour and other professors in Paris against the Dominicans and the mendicant orders in general. Cf. Neumann (1954/64: 270f.).

long as I want them, no one can destroy them.' Then I asked: 'Ah, dear Lord, shall the Order exist until the end of the world?' Then Our Lord said: 'Yes, they shall last until the end of the world. But another kind of people will come who shall instruct them, so that those who then follow shall be wiser and more powerful and have fewer earthly needs and be more fired with the Holy Spirit in the face of the wretched trouble that holy Christianity will then be facing.' Then I saw these people and their clothes and their way of life and I saw that there was a great crowd of them. They wear only two garments; the undergarment is white and the upper one red, signifying the pure humanity of Our Lord and His holy death. Their hair and their beard remain uncut. Their belt is made from the fibre of an olive tree, signifying the holy compassion they bear towards misguided Christianity. They all go barefoot, except in those places where it freezes; there they wear red shoes with white laces, but no socks. In the summer, but not in winter, they wash their heads in the forest, for they have no home of their own. They are strangers everywhere and suffer many hardships. They keep neither house nor home, silver nor gold anywhere. Each of them carries a white staff coloured with red. The staff has a crook, which is the length of one span and is of ivory. The ivory signifies that they should be chaste and pure in all things. The staff is white and red to remind them of Christ's death. The martyrdom of Our Lord is carved on one side of the staff and on the other His ascension into Heaven. They must have this staff to hand at all times, when they eat or sleep, pray or preach or sing Mass or hear confession; and when they do not have the staff in their hand, then they must stick it into the earth where they can see it so that they may have the martyrdom of Christ constantly before their eyes. If they must travel for thirty miles, either through service or need, then they must take a donkey with them in pairs, so that they may ride from time to time; when this is the case they may not carry their staff by their side, instead they must carry it before them, erect in their hand as a cross of God. They must ride this lowly animal so that they may resemble God in humility and also because their feet would become so sore that they would not be able to cover the distance. But they may only wear shoes from All Saints Day until the day that St Peter became pope.[88] They shall ask for neither breeches nor other clothes;

---

[88] That is, from 1 November till 18 January. Since 1960 the celebration of Peter's election to the position of Pope has been celebrated on 22 February (Schmidt 1995: 382, n. 176).

furthermore, if they are not offered bread then they should beg for it humbly and everything they are given, with the exception of meat, they should eat and drink in the company of the common people. They should also not fast more than Christian law prescribes and they should seek lodging that allows them to pray and sleep under a separate roof, apart from others.

When people get to know and consider this holy way of life, they will be so changed by it that, with great love, they will willingly give them what they need. Nor should these brothers lodge with any widows. The people should wash their callused feet with great tenderness, and they should give great thanks to God that the brothers go out and pour balm on misguided Christianity, just as Mary Magdalene did on Our Lord. And the people shall also pour balm on them and this shall be done by men, for the brothers are not God.[89] When people notice that their clothes are too worn they will give them new ones. If people would like to give them a lot, they should not accept it, but rather suggest that they give compassionately wherever there is a need.

Their general chapter meeting is held twice a year for the benefit and the need of Christianity, in the forest in summer and in the town, in the town hall, in winter. Any man who wants to enter this order should have two books in his possession. He shall preach out of the larger book; the first thing that is written in this book is *Credo in deum*[90] and after that it is all sermons written by masters, all ordered according to the articles of Christian faith. From the smaller book he shall observe the daily hours throughout the year in the service of Our Lord. The first master, who shall take up this way of life, shall be the son of the king of Rome. Before God his name means Alleluia.[91] The pope shall grant him his immediate authority and after that he will decide for himself and will receive from the pope this way of life.[92] Then all the great masters will join him; they shall be no younger than twenty-four years old. They will also admit no one unless they are healthy and have been educated at a school of advanced studies and they must all be priests, confessors and very distinguished teachers. They shall call their first master 'prince' and he shall be accompanied by three brothers, for in him the Christian

---

[89] Only men should wash the feet of the brothers because Christ had His feet anointed by a woman, Mary Magdalene.

[90] 'I believe in God.'

[91] On this enigmatic figure see Ancelet-Hustache (1926: 285ff.).

[92] That is, the pope will sanction the new rule.

faith shall be tested most frequently, and for every group of thirteen brothers there shall be a master, whom they shall call their overseer, and he shall be accompanied by two brothers. Their power is very great, for no bishop is their equal. Wherever they go, the right to preach, hear confession, sing and read the Mass is not denied them. In every diocese there shall be seven of them, signifying the seven gifts of the Holy Spirit; in every archdiocese there shall be thirteen, signifying the holy convocation of Our Lord.[93] In Rome there shall be thirty of them, signifying the blessed sum of money that was given for Christ. The greatest numbers will be in Jerusalem where Jesus died for us. Their small chapter meeting shall be held every three weeks, signifying the indivisible unity of the Holy Trinity, by five brothers, signifying the five wounds, or by seven, signifying the seven gifts of the Holy Spirit, and, beyond that, by as many as can come together. Wherever they eat and drink, the oldest in the order at that time shall talk a little of the way of Christ and of His holy life and the others should be silent.

I also saw their beds, how they should lie on straw between two white woollen blankets and there is a pillow for their head that is placed under the underblanket on the straw.[94] Their loins shall never sit nor lie comfortably, for they shall be vigorous all their days until holy martyrdom, as Christ was; however, all the old masters, who have been of great help and who, because of their age, cannot hold on till the end of the order without becoming weak or falling sick shall be given a comfortable bed and cared for lovingly, because they can still give much holy counsel and they shall live off the best food. This holy life shall continue in good peace for thirty years. During this time they shall so illuminate and teach Christianity that no one shall turn away from the Christian faith because of untutored ignorance.

Alas, after that the trouble will start! Then the Antichrist will arrive and will win over the worldly princes with that which is only too dear to them – gold and precious stones and endless false cunning. Thus they will follow him willingly and say that he is their god and their lord and provide him with a great retinue, their seal and their documents. Alas, then he comes to the spiritual powers! There he also finds greed and brings with him such great false wisdom that few of the bishops and provosts and priests can withstand him. Then

---

93   That is, Jesus and the twelve Apostles.

94   Cf. the description of the bed that Mechthild says Dietrich, deacon of the cathedral, should sleep in (VI, 2 [p. 108]).

these blessed brothers will hold their lives cheap and preach the Christian faith zealously and grant true absolution of all sins to those who die with true remorse in the Christian faith, so that they are saved from Purgatory. Because these holy brothers will have worked among these people in such a holy way, many holy martyrs shall stand by them. A number of Jews and some learned heathens shall receive holy baptism and the Christian faith from these brothers. This shall so incense the Antichrist that he shall impose a severe ban and exert great pressure on all those who go to hear their preaching. Whoever then goes to the brothers and stands by them is a blessed man. Thus the trouble starts. Then the good separate themselves from the bad and risk their lives and everything that they have. Then the messengers of the Antichrist arrive and their first act is to impale the holy preacher on an iron pole because of his Christian teaching; God's beloved must hang there and writhe before the poor children of God. Then they carry the holy man skewered between them for all the world to see. The wicked laugh, the good weep. Then he sings with the voice of the Holy Spirit: '*Credo in deum*',[95] and consoles and shouts out: 'Follow me, holy children of God!' All those who then follow him are taken captive, and their eyes are bound and they are beaten with whips and driven like stolen sheep to a place where water flows deeply. There, all their blessed heads are chopped off and they are thrown into the water. Where there is no water, they are driven into a field and martyred there. God inspires the wicked to blindfold the good people in order that, when they are held captive, they cannot see the great display and excessive splendour and honour, which the accursed have from the Antichrist their Lord, and so they may stand all the more firmly, for they too are only human. They take the blessed dead preacher and raise him up on high in the same place where he had preached God's word and was martyred. Those who after that would preach the Christian faith must become living martyrs and great saints.

The power of the Antichrist is so great that none can equal him. When the pope can no longer struggle against him, then he turns to the holy brothers and suffers what they suffer. Then Enoch and Elijah shall come to their aid; they are at present in sweet Paradise and live there with soul and body in the same bliss and eat the same food which would have been given to Adam had he remained there. They too, in obedience to God, must avoid that same tree, from which Eve

---

[95] 'I believe in God'.

and Adam ate the apple when they broke God's command. I have seen this tree; it is not large and its fruit has all the beauty and delight of a rose on the outside, but inside it is by nature very sour; that signifies the bitter harm of sin, which God had never wished for mankind. Since this fruit is so harmful to good people that it is still poisonous for us, God forbade it, for He never caused mankind distress.

In these final days of trouble, when these blessed brothers have consoled the people for so long that there is no good person left who has not suffered martyrdom for God, the majority of the brothers will still be alive. Then their innocent suffering is so great and their prayer is thus so holy that God then sends Enoch and Elijah to them; they shall comfort them and lead them out of the forest so that they may go and preach again and prepare themselves for death. These two lords, who then emerge from Paradise, are so wise in divine truth that they have the power to harass the Antichrist. They tell him plainly who he is, and where his extraordinary powers come from, and how he comes to be there, and what his end shall be. When the misguided hear what an accursed god has been given them because of their great greed and their delight in many kinds of evil, which God knows to be in their hearts, then many a noble man and many a lovely lady, who had left Christianity to follow the Antichrist, mend their ways. Then these blessed have to be martyred, for at that time the greatest power on earth is given to the Antichrist. He orders all the men to be rounded up whose Christian faith he can put to the test. And so boiling pans are made ready on the streets and they are all driven to them, and their wives and lovely children are sent for. Then they are made to choose whether they would prefer to keep their beautiful wives and their dear children, their wealth and honour in unbelief, or whether they would rather boil in the pans and lose their lives in Christian faith. Then the men say: 'Ah, dear women and children, don't think about me, but rather remember that you are Christians and if you sacrifice your life to God, then we shall not be parted.' Then the feet and hands of the men are bound together and they are tossed into the pans. The wives and the children too say: 'Lord Jesus, O Child of Mary, through love of You we shall willingly suffer the same torment.' And so a pit is dug and filled with fire, into which the children and the mothers are tossed, and firewood and straw are flung on top of them, and so they burn to death.

The angel escorts Enoch and Elijah out of Paradise. The radiance and the bliss, that was manifest in their bodies, must all then be left behind. When they see this Earth they are alarmed, as men are who see the sea and are worried about how they might cross it. Then they take on an earthly appearance and must then be mortal. Then they eat honey and figs and drink water mixed with wine and their spirits are also nourished by God.

IV, 28. Of the fivefold power of love. The truth must be withheld because of the frailty of people and because of the treachery of the world

This book was begun in love, it should also end in love, for there is nothing so wise, nor so holy, nor so beautiful, nor so strong, nor so perfect as love.[96] Then Our Lord Jesus Christ said: 'Speak, Father, I will now be silent as you are silent in the mouth of your Son, shaking because of the frailty of people; and in the same way my humanity spoke tremulously because of the treachery of the world, for it rewarded me with bitter death.'

---

[96] Neumann (1956/64: 216) claims that the first four books were conceived as an integrated unit by Mechthild. Cf. Kemper (1979: 96), who identifies the four emotions of 'love and desire, remorse and fear' (VI, 6, 5–6) as the principle themes of the first four books and finds a correspondence between them and the four 'stations of love' explored in the Song of Songs.

Book V

Mechthild continues her exposition of 'sinking' love with the focus here on 'sinking humility' (V, 4). Lady Love (cf. I, 1) inspires the Soul to ascend the mountain like a pilgrim; she must, however, also make the descent on the other side. After the embrace of the Holy Trinity, the Soul and Body sink into Hell, 'under Lucifer's tail'. Mechthild embraces both the ascent to the heights of Heaven and the descent to the depths of Hell as integral aspects of maturing into 'full-grown' holiness.

Although there are further lyrical exchanges in this book between God and the loving Soul (V, 17; V, 18), there is a greater emphasis on devotional instruction. Issues of self-will, free will, obedience and the nature of sin (V, 5; V, 8; V, 16) are discussed. Mechthild's sense of prophetic responsibility for the welfare of the Church emerges from her visionary experiences of Purgatory (V, 5; V, 14; V, 15). Her sense of mission is expressed in the projection of herself as a mother to three groups of sinful 'children' who are in need of support and correction (V, 8). For Mechthild the Virgin Mary is the model of motherhood. Mechthild's engagement with Mary in four visions (I, 22; II, 4; VII, 60 and here V, 23) reveals most clearly that fusion of mystical experience and salvation history which is conceptually so fundamental to the character of her writings.

The continued anxieties which Mechthild has about her identity as author are addressed in dialogue with God (V, 12; V, 32). She learns that her book is intended to be a messenger of God, fulfilling the same function as contemporary saints (V, 34) and sharing the purpose of the prophets in the Bible (V, 12). The immanence of God in Mechthild's writings is conveyed by a resumption of the earlier allegorisation of her book (II, 26).

V, 4. The power of wondrous love is manifold; how the Soul sinks. Of four kinds of humility. Of seven aspects of the beauty of the loving Soul

O wondrous Love of God, you have great and holy power, you illumine the Soul and instruct the Senses and endow all virtues with full strength. What good fortune for the poor peasant that I am, that I ever caught sight of you, Lady! Ah Love, you are full of delight and worthy of praise in all that you do, I know this in my soul; all virtues are subject to you. But the two virtues, both equally pure, that must accompany love and yet shall always be subordinate to it are sinking humility, that is not tainted by arrogance in the spiritual life, and chastity, innate or acquired.

This Love moves through the Senses and storms the Soul with all its virtues. As Love grows in the Soul, so she ascends in desire to God and extends herself, flowing towards the wonder that comes to meet her. She melts through the Soul into the Senses; thus the Body must also have its share so that it becomes refined in all things.

Is it possible to have bad habits if one lives in the love of God? I can find no evidence of this; the sincere love of God has such great power. However, the Soul is never so flooded with the love of God that she is not often tempted by earthly things; the Soul that is permeated by false love is not receptive to this love. When Love is full-grown in the Soul she has also ascended as far as is humanly possible, for Love is measured in her ordering. If she did not have measure, o sweet God, how many pure hearts would burst in sweet bliss.

When the Soul, with the upward flight of love and the great desire of her heart in her pursuit of God, has reached the summit of the high mountain of mighty love and blissful knowledge, she behaves like the pilgrim who has climbed mountains with great eagerness but descends on the other side very anxious lest he lose his footing. So it is for the Soul: when she has been so flooded with light in the heat of long love and has become so overpowered in the embrace of the Holy Trinity, she then begins to sink and to cool, as does the sun when it drops from its zenith and sinks down into the night. God knows, this is what happens to the Soul and also to the Body. The Soul, rich in love, sinks, drawn by boundless humility, and constantly pulls back from what God does for her out of love; she is very content with this because of the noble nature that fills God and herself with the same will. And so the Soul turns the eye of its pleasure from all things so that she might win much praise for God. The Body also sinks deeply whenever it serves its enemy and silently obeys and avoids its friends to honour God. The Soul sinks down even further, for she has greater power than the Body. She sinks with great eagerness into the lowest place that God has in His power. Oh, how do I dare to name this place to those who are ignorant of sinking humility.

The first humility is to be seen in the home and in clothes, which are appropriate and are cut and sewn as befits a religious person and are also clean. The second humility is to be found in conduct towards others that is loving in all difficult circumstances and in all things. The holy love of God will grow from this. The third humility is to be found in the Senses when a person employs them in all things appropriately and loves in an ordered way. The fourth humility lives in the Soul; this is sinking humility that works so many sweet wonders in the Soul rich in love. It chases the Soul up into Heaven and draws her back down into the abyss; it leads the Soul to all creatures individually and says: 'Now see, all this is better than you are!' and brings her to that place where she can sink no deeper, that is under Lucifer's tail. In her desire to honour God she would like nothing better than to stay there, if she could. The poor Soul rich in love is so bound[97] by humble Love that she is not ashamed and only fears as is appropriate in Heaven. But the poor Body must fear and be ashamed of both the darkness of its heart and the weakness of its external senses, because it has not yet been transformed by death.

However, the Soul is just as beautiful in her body as she is in Heaven, but she is not as secure; she is just as bold, but not as strong; she is just as powerful, but not so constant; she is just as full of love, but not as happy; she is just as generous, but not so rich; she is just as holy, but not as innocent; she is just as satisfied, but not so contented. This is true only of the Soul that is here flooded with the humble love of God.

When the Soul has thus ascended to the height of what is accessible to her while she is still yoked to her body, and has sunk to the lowest depth she can find, then she is full-grown[98] in virtue and in holiness. She must then be adorned with the suffering of long waiting.

Thus the Soul takes up her position in loyal stance
And observes all things with great wisdom;
Thus nothing can escape her
From which she may draw praise for God.

V, 5. Of the purgatory of a beguine, whom no prayer could help because of her self-will

Alas, Sin, that you are so harmful, since even holy deeds are harmful if done without guidance, when, for example, one says: No, I have no need for human counsel, I want to live according to God's counsel. These words have always filled me with horror, for no one anywhere

---

97 On Mechthild's concept of 'bound' and 'unbound' love, cf. II, 24 (p. 47).
98 Cf. I, 44 (p. 35) in which the Soul is described as a 'full grown bride'.

may humble himself more usefully than in following Christian counsel with an obedient heart. I observed this in a woman; she loved Our Lord from the bottom of her heart and she worked on this love with such superhuman effort that her physical being withered to the extent that death was inevitable. Then, according to Christian custom,[99] I prayed for her. In my rapt spirit I saw her spirit that in itself was as clear as the sun. This was because of the faithful intention of her pure heart. She was enveloped in a great darkness and wanted so much to reach the eternal light. The dark night was always in front of her whenever she was on the ascent; it was self-will without guidance that hindered this virtuous person so much. I asked her: 'How can you be helped?' Then she replied as follows: 'On Earth I did not want to follow, in accordance with Christian ordinance, the counsel of anyone. For this reason no one's prayer or wish may help me.' Then I turned to Our dear Lord and asked Him how it could be that a person could find themselves in torment, who on Earth had accepted such holy suffering for His sake. Then Our Lord said: 'All virtues are nothing to me that are not informed by counsel, for I came to Earth through counsel[100] and on Earth I served my Father and all people in great subservience and then I ascended into Heaven in complete freedom; but no one followed me in what I always did. When she goes to Heaven she will be adorned with the wishes, prayers and all the deeds done on her behalf here.' The Soul: 'For everything that is given to us as help on the path to the Kingdom of Heaven is ours by right. However, when we arrive there it is for all souls. God does this for us out of love that they might more readily come and help us to praise God in eternal honour.' By rights, the sufferings of this beguine should have lasted seventeen years, but God in His mercy reduced this to just seventeen months, because she had acted out of such heartfelt love. May God help us to find the right measure. Amen!

V, 8. The good person shall have three children for whom he shall pray

No one knows what consolation or suffering or desire is unless he has himself been touched by these three; I am looking for help, for I am

---

99   Cf. V, 15 (p. 92); VII, 41 (p. 134).
100 This is a reference to the visionary account Mechthild gives of the two councils held by the Trinity (III, 9 [pp. 58ff.]), one of which resulted in the creation of mankind and the other in the descent of the Son to earth to redeem mankind.

unfortunately in great pain. I have three children whom I see in great distress.

The poor sinners are the first child, who rest in eternal death; their only consolation is that they still have their human body.[101] Alas, I look at this child with a bleeding heart and, with weeping eyes, take it into the arms of my soul and carry it to the feet of its Father, from whom I have it. Then I look at this child and beg its faithful Father, Jesus, to arouse it with the same voice of divine mercy with which He awoke Lazarus. To this God replies thus: 'I will cure this child of its sickness; if it chooses not to fall into this death again, it shall be like me in my beauty, my nobility, my wealth, surrounded and suffused with all pleasure in this eternal eternity. Rise up my dear child, you are cured! The free will, which I have given you, I shall never take away from you, because, as for the saints, it shall be the measure of all your worth in the splendid Kingdom of Heaven.' Alas, the child still lies motionless on its own self-will!

The poor souls who are tormented in Purgatory are my second child; I must give them blood from my heart to drink. When I intercede for them and contemplate the many kinds of distress and the bitter thirst that they suffer for every single sin, then I feel a mother's sorrow. And yet I am pleased that they suffer just pain to honour God. They suffer their torments with great patience, for they see all their guilt clearly. They suffer their distress in disciplined wisdom and drink deeply of their heart's sorrow. If this child is to recover quickly, then the mother must be very faithful and merciful.

The imperfect religious are my third child. When I look at all my sick children there is none that distresses me more than this one in particular, because it has, unfortunately, distanced itself so far and so much from heavenly things through the absorption of its external senses in temporal things that it has altogether lost the noble way of life and sweet intimacy with God, for which God had chosen it specially. They have all gone so badly astray that no one can bring them back to the right path with words. And so they deride the inner life and pervert the sweetness of God and interpret everything they see and hear falsely. Thus, outwardly they appear wise, but, unfortunately, are fools inwardly. This child is the most difficult one to cure, for it falls first of all into self-willed conflict, after that into lethargy, after that into false consolation, after that into despondency, after that it is unfortunately devoid of all grace. In this way, this poor child

---

[101]   That is, they are spiritually moribund, though not yet physically dead.

struggles on in a sinful life until its death. And so it is impossible to tell where this lost soul might end up.

V, 12. How God replies to a brother about what is written in this book

Master Heinrich,[102] you are surprised by some of the words written in this book. I am surprised that you are surprised. What is more, I have been greatly troubled in my heart since that time when I, a sinful woman, was obliged to write, for I am unable to express the true knowledge and the holy, glorious revelations to anyone other than in these words; measured against the eternal truth, they seem to me far too inadequate.

I asked the eternal Master what He had to say about this. Then He answered thus: 'Ask him how it came about that the Apostles, who had been so timorous, became so bold when they received the Holy Spirit.[103] Ask him further where Moses was when he saw nothing but God.[104] And also ask him, how it was that Daniel, as a child, spoke.'[105]

V, 14. Of the purgatory of unworthy priests

A long time ago I saw a purgatory;[106] it had the appearance of fiery water and it bubbled like fiery, molten bell metal and a dark pall hung over it. There were fish swimming in the water that had a human likeness. These were the souls of wretched priests, who in this world had swum in the greed of all desire and who had been on fire here with accursed lust, which blinds them to the extent that they can love nothing good. There were fishermen on the water; they had neither boat nor net, instead they fished with their fiery claws for

---

102 The *Ld* identifies Heinrich further as Brother Heinrich of Halle, lector at Ruppin. Cf. Introduction (p. 9).

103 Cf. Acts 2: 3–7.

104 Cf. Exodus 3: 6.

105 The Book of Susanna (one of the smaller books of the Apocrypha) tells of the false accusation of adultery brought against Susanna by two elders, her condemnation, but then her deliverance by the sagacity of the child Daniel. The *Ld* concludes the chapter with more information about Heinrich of Halle. We are told that he collected all Mechthild's writings together in one volume and ordered them into six parts (cf. Introduction, p. 9). We are also told of a vision that Mechthild has of Heinrich's soul in the presence of God, holding Mechthild's book in his hand and how he has been rewarded for his work on the book.

106 In medieval visionary literature, unlike Heaven and Hell, Purgatory had no fixed geographical location. In referring to 'a purgatory' Mechthild seems to be indicating that in her universe there was more than one place of purgatory. Cf. Bochsler (1997: 98f.).

they were both spirits and devils. When they had landed the souls, embittered, they skinned them and tossed them straight into a boiling pot; there they poked at them with fiery pitchforks. When they were cooked through to their liking, then they gobbled them down through their beaks. Then they went back out on the water again and excreted them through their tails and fished them and boiled them and devoured them again.

V, 15. Of the purgatory of a worthy priest

A pure priest died in his own rightful parish. Then I prayed for him, as one does on behalf of another according to Christian custom.[107] Then my soul saw his in splendid dignity, while he was still waiting for heavenly honour. Four angels led him through all the turbulence in the first heaven and they played to him on heavenly lyres. This was his purgatory with which they prepared him for heavenly bliss. I asked him how he had come to be so greatly honoured. Then he said: 'On Earth I loved solitude and was only afraid in my prayer.' Then I said: 'Ah, you very blessed man, why did you not ascend immediately to Heaven with these rapturous angels?' Then he spoke again thus: 'The honour that I shall receive for my pure ministry is so great that I may not go there yet.'

V, 16. It is devilish to sin

There are some educated people who say that to sin is human. In all the temptation of my sinful body and in all the emotion of my heart and in all the knowledge of my senses and in all the nobility of my soul, it has always been my experience that the committing of a sin is devilish. Whether the sin be great or small, the Devil is always its companion. What is more, the devilishness that we acquire of our own free will is in itself more harmful than all the rest of our human condition. This is human: hunger, thirst, heat, cold, suffering, sorrow, temptation, sleep, weariness; these are the things that Christ suffered, who was truly human for us and with us. And so if sin were solely a human matter, then He would have had to sin too, for He was a true man in body and a just man in wisdom and a constant man in virtue and a perfect man in the Holy Spirit, and beyond that He was eternal God in eternal truth and not a sinner. However, if we would be like Him, then we must also live like Him or be redeemed through repentance.

[107] Cf. V, 5 (p. 89); VII, 41 (p. 134).

V, 17. The greeting, praise and prayer of the sinner
'Greetings to You, living God, You are mine above all things. It is an endless source of joy to me that I may speak to You openly. When my enemies pursue me then I flee into Your arms, where I can give vent to my suffering while You incline yourself towards me. You know well how to pluck the strings of my soul;[108] ah, begin immediately, that You may be ever blessed. I am an unworthy bride, yet You are my rightful Lover; I shall rejoice in this forever. Remember how You may caress the pure Soul in Your lap and do so now, Lord, even though I am unworthy of You. Ah Lord, if You draw me up to You, I become pure and radiant. If You leave me in myself then I remain in darkness and heaviness.'

V, 18. How God replies to this
This is how God replies: 'My greeting to you in response is such a great flood from Heaven that were I to enter into you without restraint, that would be the end of your earthly life. So you see, I must hold back my might and cloak my radiance, so that I may keep you longer in the misery of this Earth until all my sweetness shall rise to the heights of my eternal glory, and my strings shall sound sweetly for you, as befits the faithful worth of your abiding love. However, I shall make a start and tune my heavenly strings in your soul so that you may be able to wait longer; for the preparation of illustrious brides and noble knights is a long, intensive and costly process.'

V, 23. Of Mary's prayer, of Gabriel's light, of the Child's blanket, where the milk came from, of the gifts for the Child, of the devils and the Hunger Cloth
I saw a maiden at her prayer. Her body was inclined towards the earth and her spirit had raised itself towards the eternal Godhead; for before the time that Jesus Christ unlocked Heaven with the key of the holy cross, there was never anyone so holy that his spirit would or could rise up through effort and soar with desire and embrace the Holy Trinity with love in the eternal heights. The spirit of the pure virgin could not enter Heaven because Adam had pushed the bolt too tightly shut. However, from time to time God inclined Himself so close to the earth that He comforted His friends and they understood His will. But the prophets cried out loudly and implored Our Lord to

---

108 For Mechthild's use of the imagery of stringed music, cf. I, 2 (p. 28); II, 2 (p. 38); III, 9 (p. 58); V, 18 (p. 93).

come down here. However, it was this virgin who drew Our Lord down with the sweet voice of her soul, and she spoke thus in her prayer when she was alone: 'Lord God, I rejoice that You will come in such a noble fashion, that a maiden shall be Your mother. Lord, with my purity and with all that I have from You, I offer myself in service.'

Then the angel Gabriel descended in a heavenly light. The virgin was bathed in the light and the angel wore clothing the like of which I have never seen on earth. When she saw the light with the eyes of her body, then she stood up and was afraid. When she looked at the angel she found the likeness of her purity in his face. Then she stood very demurely and inclined her ear and lifted up her senses. Then the angel greeted her and made God's will known to her. These words of his were dear to her heart and her senses became full and her soul fiery. However, she asked for an explanation; it was her maidenly modesty and divine love that drove her to this. When she had been enlightened, she opened up her heart in good will and with all her might. Then she knelt down and said: 'I give myself in service to God in accordance with your words.'[109]

Then the complete Holy Trinity, with the power of the Godhead and with the good will of its Humanity and with the noble gracefulness of the Holy Spirit, passed right through her virginal body into the fiery soul of her good will and settled itself in the open heart of her most pure flesh and fused itself with everything that it found in her, so that her flesh became Its flesh, so that He, a perfect child, grew in her body and so that she became a true mother of His flesh and remained a maiden intact. And the longer she carried Him, the more radiant, the more beautiful and wiser she became. Then she stood up and said: 'Lord Father, I praise You, for You have magnified me and my family shall be magnified in Heaven and on Earth.' When the time came round that other women are in low spirits and walk with difficulty, Mary, by contrast, was light-footed and joyful. Yet her body was fully extended, for she had within her the perfectly formed Son of God. Mary did not know when God wished to be born of her before she saw Him in her lap on the road, on that night in Bethlehem, in that unfamiliar town and where she herself was a poor stranger without lodging. Almighty God with His wisdom, the eternal Son with His human truth, the Holy Spirit with His tender sweetness passed effortlessly in flowing bliss through the intact

---

[109] Cf. Luke 1: 38.

body of Mary. And that happened as quickly as when the sun shines in loving calm after the sweet dew.[110]

When Mary saw her beautiful Child, then she inclined her head to his face and said: 'Welcome, my innocent Child and my mighty Lord, all things are Yours.' At the conception of Our Lord and in the pregnancy of His mother and at His birth and in the lap of His mother, before He was put in the crib, the power of the Holy Trinity and the blissful fire of Heaven burnt so strongly in Mary that the spirit of Hell, that traverses all the world and knows all that goes on, could not get near enough to the country and the place, where Mary was, to learn the miracle of how the Child had arrived here. Mary took from Joseph's saddle a rough blanket that the donkey wore on its back under the saddle, and also the upper part of her shift, under which she had carried Our Lord. The other part she wrapped around her body again. The slight Virgin wrapped the mighty Saviour in this material and laid Him in the crib; then He cried immediately like any new-born child; as long as children have no speech they never cry without due cause. And so Our Lord did when, despite His noble nature, He was given such a rough bed in a byre because of wicked sin; then He wept for all mankind. Then He hid all His glory and all His might. Then the Virgin was distressed and the Child became hungry and cold.

Then the Mother had to nurse her son; that was His Father's will and the Holy Spirit's desire. Then the Virgin, in motherly love and maidenly modesty, leaned over her distressed Child and offered Him her young breast. Now hear wonders! The bright blooming[111] of her beautiful eyes and the spiritual beauty of her maidenly face and the flowing sweetness of her pure heart and the joyous sparkling of her noble soul, these four things came together in her maidenly breast according to the will of the Father and the need of the Son and the desire of the Holy Spirit. Then the sweet milk flowed from her pure heart without any pain. Then the Child sucked as a human infant and His mother rejoiced reverently. The angels sang a hymn of praise to God. The shepherds came, they sought and found, swaddled in the crib of a stranger for all to see, our true pledge of redemption. Then I asked Mary where Joseph was. Then she said: 'He has gone into town and is buying some small fish and plain bread for us', and they drank water too. Then I said: 'Ah, Lady, you should eat the very best

[110] Cf. I, 22 (p. 30, n. 9).
[111] Cf. I, 2 (p. 28, n. 5).

bread and drink the finest wine.' 'No', she said, 'that is the rich man's food, we don't have any of that in this poor life.'

When the strange star appeared, then Satan also came to Beth-lehem and followed the Three Kings swiftly and he looked at the Child with great malice. When they honoured the Child so highly with great gifts, then Satan's thoughts were thrown into confusion and this is what he said to himself: 'What has happened to you now, you unfortunate wretch, this may well be that same Child of Whom the prophets wrote, Whose birth Lucifer charged you long and repeatedly with attending, that you might defile it; for then all the wide world would reside with us in Hell. This Child has been conceived and born without sin, otherwise it would never have been hidden from me. Now all my cunning has been in vain. Now I must return to my master and lament this disaster, for this Child will become too mighty for us. If He triumphs over us, how shall we bear that? Never before has any child been born that was shown such honour.' When Lucifer heard this news, the archfiend sat and gnashed his teeth and howled so that the fire of his anger lit up the whole of Hell. Then he spoke thus: 'Should a man become our judge, then we must for evermore tremble before all those people who live according to His will. Go back there, Satan, and enlist the help of the princes of the land, the masters of the Jews, and teach them how they must kill Him in His infancy before He goes to school.' When Satan came to Herod he found Lucifer's likeness in this corrupt man: hate, pride, greed. By these three paths the great devil infiltrated Herod's large heart and spread into all his five senses and made the king so murderous that he carried out the devil's will on the innocent chil-dren, who are now honoured saints in Heaven.

I asked Mary what she had done with the gifts since she had not bought herself a lamb to sacrifice.[112] Then she said: 'Holy flowing generosity and compassion for those in need and the love of volun-tary poverty, these have stripped me of my treasure. My sacrificial lamb was Jesus Christ, Son of the almighty God, who was born out of my heart and Whom all the spotless lambs signify who were ever sacrificed and brought to honour in accordance with the spirit of His father; He is my true sacrificial lamb, I should not have any other. With the gifts that were brought to my Child, I have cared for all those whom I found truly in need. These were impoverished orphans and pure virgins, who could be given a dowry so that they need not be

---

112   That is, the gifts of the Three Kings. Cf. Luke 2: 22–24.

stoned[113] and, in addition to them, the sick who had been abandoned and those greatly advanced in years; they were to benefit from it, for God had reserved it for them. After the real need of these poor people, I had thirty gold marks left; I was to spend these on a Hunger Cloth to which ordinary people went to pray, for it held great meaning.[114]

The cloth was half-black and half-white. The side of the cloth that faced north in the temple was black; that was the long darkness of the Old Testament. Green pictures were embroidered on it; for although the Old Testament was darkened by many great sins, there were nevertheless some people at that time who did not wither because of their sins, rather they were dark because of what the Law demanded of them. The images depicted were all to do with the guilt and the distress that moved mighty God so much that He preserved Noah, that righteous man, with his household and let the rest of the world perish. To the south in the house of prayer the Cloth was a noble white. That signified the pure, radiant chastity of St Mary, with which we shall all overcome all the sorrow of our heart. There were pictures embroidered in gold, which represented the birds that Noah sent out from the ark and which signified the faithless greedy, who seek all their comfort here on Earth. But there was also embroidered on it the pure dove with a green twig, that returned in innocence without having taken carrion flesh into its mouth. By this, all those were to be understood who come daily to God with new virtues and who maintain themselves, drawn by the Holy Spirit, in the flight to Heaven. Down the length of the Cloth, where the pieces were joined, there was a golden strip. Across the Cloth in the centre there was green braid, studded with precious stones. This signified the most noble wood that carried Our Lord's body when the gates of Heaven were breached and battered open with hammers so that Adam's bolt flew off. Though few understood the significance, these two pieces of decoration formed a splendid cross. There was a white sacrificial

---

113 The *Ld* glosses this further by saying that these women were given dowries so that they would not, in accordance with the law, be stoned as adulteresses. Schmidt (1995: 387f., n. 207) points to a possible allusion to the legend of St Nicholas. Nicholas gave money to a poor father with three daughters so that they would not be sold to the whorehouse.

114 The Hunger Cloth was a piece of material that, in earlier times, was hung in front of the altar or the Choir as a symbol of mourning and penance during Lent. It was often embroidered with images and patterns of symbolic meaning. Cf. Schmidt (1995: 388, n. 208).

lamb embroidered on the cross and it was adorned with precious stones and with gold so bright it looked as if it was on fire. This foretold, as it came about, that the innocent Lamb of God suffered through love a great death on the tall tree. The reason that the lifeless Hunger Cloth with the lifeless lamb fell to the ground in the martyrdom of Our Lord was that the living Lamb of God might be worshipped for ever in that same place. Mary sewed for her child Jesus a gown with a special seam that could be let out and lengthened when the gown became tight and short. The gown was pale brown and made of rough twisted yarn. Joseph was a poor man's carpenter, so he earned some pennies to meet their needs. Mary sewed and spun, making clothes for the three of them. When they fled into Egypt the angel of God cloaked them in a heavenly light so that the Devil did not know where the child was until He had reached the age of thirty and was a perfect man. The Devil became aware of Him in the desert and after that on a number of occasions through miraculous signs. Then Satan turned to the Jewish masters who were outwardly splendid in demeanour, but inwardly corrupt. He taught them how they should resist Jesus with perverted words and how they should never accept His teachings and thus how they could hold to their Jewish law. Then Satan went to Lucifer again and said: 'Alas master, our honour is doomed! I have found a man on sinful earth who on his own is stronger and wiser than all of us put together before our Fall, for with all my powers I cannot bring him to a single sinful thought.' Then Lucifer howled again like a hound and gnashed his hellish fangs and said: 'You must oppose Him with all mankind. If He is the greatest of all men then He will be able to escape all sin.' 'Master, we'll get ourselves out of this trouble, for I shall find plenty of people who would willingly kill this Man.' Then he said: 'No, I fear that it will probably not go well for us, for, with the supreme power of God, He saves so quickly from the temptations of the flesh and from mortal death. Were His life to be taken from Him, I have an even greater fear that His soul would come among us and rescue His own; for it is far beyond our power that, in defiance of nature, He can save people on Earth from all sorts of suffering in death; however, because of original sin, He must Himself descend to Hell. But if He remains free of all sin and His life is taken from Him, though He is innocent, then He will not belong to Hell, for never was angel or man damned who was guiltless; then He alone will be noble and free and whatever He wants shall happen regardless of us. However, with a little cunning you can arrange it that the great majority belongs with us in Hell. But you must always see to it that He is humiliated in the extreme and that He is tormented with the sharpest of pains. If He is pure man then He might fall into despair and so remain with us.'

Mary, Our Lady, spoke in her thoughts to Our Lord as often as she needed and sometimes His Godhead would answer her and enable her to bear the sorrow of her heart with composure; Mary Magdalene was not at all prepared in this way – when she did not see Our Lord with the eyes of her body,[115] she was inconsolable and during that time her heart was burdened with great distress and pain. She burned in simple love without any higher knowledge of heavenly things until the hour when the Apostles received the Holy Spirit;[116] then for the first time her soul was wounded by the Godhead. Our Lady, however, was very quiet when Our Lord rose from the dead so gloriously, yet of all mankind her heart had the most profound knowledge of God.

V, 32. Of the exalted end of Sister Mechthild

Now I am compelled to write down these words nevertheless, which I would gladly keep to myself, were it not that I am afraid of the surreptitious blow of vainglory. But, if God is to be just towards me, I am even more afraid that I, poor woman of God, have kept too much to myself. Since childhood I have borne misery, fear and constant heartache for the sake of a good end. Now God has shown me very recently how two hosts, they were virgins and angels, came down from Heaven in a procession. The virgins signify those virtues with which a person has served God; the angels signify a pure life with which a person has followed God.

Our Lord and His glorious Mother followed the blissful procession until those at the head were standing directly in front of the person; the way was peaceful, and on all sides the radiance of the saints was brighter than the sun, because they came from the bliss of God. Then the Soul said: 'Lord, this way delights me well beyond what I deserve. But I am very concerned about how I shall be separated from my body.' Then Our Lord said: 'When it is time, I shall breathe you in so that you are drawn to me as to a magnet.'

On both sides of the procession there was a throng of devils; there were so many of them that I could not take them all in; however, I had no fear of any of them. They hit one another with great ferocity and they clawed one another as if demented. The Soul rejoiced all the more when she saw Our Lord before her. Then, greatly astonished, she asked Our Lord why this was so. Then Our Lord said: 'The joy

---

[115] Cf. John 20: 1 and the Interpretive Essay, p. 148.
[116] Cf. Acts 2: 1–4.

comes from the absolute certainty of knowing that none of these devils may ever separate you from me.'

V, 34. Of five new saints, sent because of unworthy people, and how God will wash Christianity in His own blood afterwards

Given the nobility that is inherent in holiness and the weakness inherent in mankind, I am greatly astonished that St Elisabeth,[117] who had not been long under the sod, became a saint so quickly. Our Lord explained this to me and said: 'It is right for messengers to be swift. Elisabeth is and was a messenger whom I sent to impious women, who sat in castles, so steeped in unchastity and so covered in pride and so constantly surrounded by vanity that by rights they should have gone into the abyss. Many ladies have followed her example, in as far as they could and wanted to. I sent St Dominic[118] as a messenger to the unbelievers and as a teacher to the ignorant and as a comforter to the distressed. I also sent St Francis[119] as a messenger to greedy priests and arrogant laymen. And St Peter,[120] the new martyr, is my messenger of blood, in which heretical Christianity is now so wretchedly steeped. They all say they are pure, and in my eyes they are impure. They say they are faithful, and yet in my eyes they are false. They say I am dear to them, their flesh is far dearer to them. Whoever would stay with me should renounce his earthly body with St Peter. Concealed guilt becomes in the end public distress.'

Poor wretch that I am, I became so bold in my prayer that I dared to take the whole of corrupt Christianity on the arm of my soul; I supported her with difficulty. Then Our Lord said: 'Leave her, she's too heavy for you.' 'Alas no, sweet Lord, I want to lift her up and carry her to Your feet with Your own arms, as You carried her on the cross.' Then God let me, poor wretch, have my way so that He might quiet me. When pitiful Christianity came thus before Our Lord she resembled a young lady. Then I looked at her and I saw too that Our

---

117 Elisabeth of Thuringia, daughter of King Andreas II of Hungary, lived from 1207 till 1231 and was canonised in 1235.

118 Dominic (1170–1221), born into the old Castilian family of Guzman, was the founder of the Order of Preachers and was canonised in 1234.

119 Francis (1182–1226), born in Assisi as Johannes, but named Francis because of his love of the French language and chivalric culture, was the founder of the Franciscan Order and was canonised in 1228.

120 Peter Martyr (1205–52), born in Verona, joined the Dominicans in 1221, studied in Bologna and preached against the heresies of the Cathars in Lombardy and Tuscany. He was murdered by heretics and canonised in 1253.

Lord was looking at her. Then I was greatly ashamed. Then Our Lord said: 'Now look! Is it fitting for me to love this young lady for ever in my eternal bridal bed[121] and to take her to me in my majestic arms and to look at her with my divine eyes, for the eyes of her knowledge are misted over and furthermore her hands are crippled, because she hardly does any good deeds? The feet of her desire are also lame, because she thinks about me rarely and reluctantly. Nor is her skin clear, because she is impure and unchaste.' Then the poor spirit said: 'How may she best be advised?' Then Our Lord said: 'I will wash her in my own blood and all the blessed who are truly innocent I shall protect and take them to me secretly in a holy death.' Our Lord said further: 'I have sent Sister Jutta of Sangerhausen[122] with her holy prayers and her good example as a messenger to the heathen.'

Our Lord also said: 'This book I now send as a messenger to all religious people, both the unworthy and the worthy, for, if the pillars collapse, then the building cannot remain standing. I tell you truly,' said Our Lord, 'this book is written in the blood of my heart that I shall shed once more at the end of time.' Our Lord told me about three kinds of blood as follows: The first blood, shed by Abel and the innocent children,[123] by John the Baptist and all those whose holy, innocent blood was spilt before the passion of Our Lord, was Christ's blood, because they suffered a blessed death through His love. The second blood was that of the Heavenly Father, which Christ poured out of His innocent heart. The third blood, which shall be shed in Christian faith before the Day of Judgement, is the blood of the Holy Spirit, for no good deed was ever accomplished without the help of the Holy Spirit. The blood of those who were martyred for the sake of Christ offers communion and a crown. The Father's blood in Christ offers salvation and faith. The last blood in the Holy Spirit offers redemption and honour.

---

121 Cf. p. 30, n. 7.
122 Jutta of Sangerhausen became a nun after her husband had died on a pilgrimage to Palestine and her children had entered the religious life. Like Elisabeth of Thuringia, she worked amongst the poor and lepers. She was never canonised but was venerated as a saint in Prussia where she was engaged in missionary work from 1260 as a hermitess. She died in 1264. Cf. Schmidt 1995: 390, n. 231.
123 That is, the Holy Innocents whom Herod had put to death.

Book VI

Although Mechthild continues to report visions of cosmic significance, most notably a further apocalyptic vision (VI, 15), there is a greater engagement in this book with her contemporary context and mundane affairs. The book opens with a chapter (VI, 1) of practical and pragmatic advice addressed to those in authority over others in the religious life. It would seem that Mechthild had some responsibility herself for fellow beguines (VI, 7). The regard in which Mechthild was held as an intercessor by some of her contemporaries is evident in the advice Dietrich, the newly appointed deacon of Magdeburg cathedral, seeks from God through Mechthild (VI, 2). The tone of harsh criticism of the cathedral clergy by God (VI, 3) is reiterated by Mechthild in a fierce attack in her own right on those priests who are unworthy of their calling (VI, 21).

Two chapters (VI, 31; VI, 36) offer a tantalising glimpse into the contemporary reception of Mechthild's writings in some quarters, as Mechthild responds to criticism levelled at earlier pieces (I, 44; II, 4). The reasonable and persuasive tone she adopts in VI, 31 gives way to a fiery response in VI, 36, revealing a much more spirited nature than her earlier self-projection as a humble, fearful and insecure woman would suggest. In VI, 36, as in VI, 23, Mechthild insists, once more, on the validity and authority of the apprehension of divine knowledge through the spiritual senses. Towards the end of the book there is a world-weary tone in Mechthild's appeal to God to release her from the constant attacks she has endured from her enemies (VI, 38). By contrast, in an address to her fellow beguines (VI, 41), or possibly nuns at this stage, we are aware of an eager readership, whose expectations, however, Mechthild does not feel able to meet. The earlier conflict between the Body and the Soul gives way to a more reconciliatory attitude in the joyful anticipation of the afterlife (VI, 35).

VI, 1. Of how a prior or prioress or other prelates should behave towards those in their care

There is much to be feared about power. Whenever someone says: 'You are now our prelate or our prior or our prioress', God knows, my friend, then you will be tested to the limit. So you should prostrate

yourself with great humility and then begin to pray immediately and
let God comfort you. Then you should so transform your heart in the
holy love of God that you love each brother or sister in your care individually in all their needs. You should be lovingly cheerful or
earnestly kind towards your subordinates and brothers, and you
should be compassionate towards them in all their work, and with
warm words you should bid them go and preach boldly and hear
confessions courageously,[124] for God has sent them into the world
that they might be the redeemers and helpers of poor sinners in the
same way as Christ was the Redeemer of all the world and descended
here into the mire of this world from the palace on high of the Holy
Trinity.

To each one of the brothers you should speak thus with the boundless humility of your pure heart: 'Ah, my friend, I, who am unworthy
of all that is good, am your servant in every way I can be and not your
master. However, unfortunately, you are in my charge and I send you
forth with the heartfelt love of God. I feel for you greatly in your
work, but it is for me to make the decisions: I rejoice in the exalted
honour that the heavenly Father has prepared for you.

Now I send you out in the same name in which Jesus took leave of
His Father, when He sought so long for the lost sheep that He died of
love. May the true love of God accompany you in holy ways and in
good works. I will send the desire of my soul and the prayer of my
heart and the tears of my sinful eyes with you, that, for my sake, God
may return you to me blessed and full of love, amen.'

You should comfort all your brothers in this way when they set
out. You should also gladden them whenever they return. You should
go to the guesthouse ahead of them and, with the generosity of God
and to the best of your ability, should see to it as far as possible that
all the needs of God's disciples are met comfortably. Ah, friend, you
should wash their feet yourself – you will still remain their master or
mistress – and place yourself humbly at their service. You should not
spend too much time with the guests, you should keep the convent in
good order. The guests should not keep a long vigil, that is, a holy
matter. You should visit the infirmary every day and soothe the sick
with the comforting words of God and care for them generously with
earthly things, for the wealth of God is beyond all counting. You
should do the cleaning for the sick and should laugh sweetly with
them in God. You should attend to their personal needs yourself and

---

[124] Cf. III, 1 (p. 54) and IV, 27 (p. 82).

ask them in faith and in love what their individual illness is and stand by them steadfastly. Then God's sweetness will flow wonderfully into you.

You should also go into the kitchen and see to it that the food for the brothers is sufficiently good, so that neither your meanness nor the cook's laziness robs Our Lord of sweet singing in the choir, for a famished priest never sings well; nor can a hungry man study deeply; this is how God must often lose the best through the worst.

In the chapter meetings you should be just with sweet temper and, in this spirit, judge fairly according to guilt. You should take great care not to assert your authority over the will of the brothers or the will of the convent, for that leads to great discord.

You should always cross yourself against those proud thoughts that, unfortunately, invade the heart in the guise of goodness saying: 'Yes, you are prior or prioress over them all, you may certainly do what seems right to you.' No, my friend, in this way you disturb the holy peace of God. In a submissive manner and in loving joy you should say this: 'Dear brother or sister, how does this please you?' and then act in accordance with their best intentions.

When the brothers or sisters of your convent offer you honour, then you should fear inwardly, keeping a sharp eye on your heart, and outwardly you should express your shame in a disciplined manner. You should receive all complaints mercifully and give all counsel faithfully.

If your brothers want to build great buildings, you should turn that to holy advantage and speak thus: 'Ah very dear brothers, let us build a marvellous palace for the Holy Trinity in our soul with the timber of Holy Scripture and with the stones of noble virtues.' Boundless humility is the cornerstone of this glorious palace, in which eternal God shall unceasingly caress his eager Bride meeting the need of His powerful desire and her great longing. This stone has been so well cut with the sweet sufficiency of earthly transience that greedy arrogance and sharp vainglory shall never bring us to build as earthly lords or ladies; rather we want to build as heavenly princes on earth. Then, on the Day of Judgement, we shall sit like the holy Apostles next to poor Jesus. Dear brothers, we want to build our dwelling in Heaven with divine joy and we want to build our refuge on earth with care, for we have no certainty that we shall live until tomorrow.

You should have the eye of an eagle and pay attention to and look at those in your charge not harshly, but lovingly in God. If you find someone who is secretly tempted, then, oh, stand by him most lovingly. Then God cannot help but be close to you.

I want to address the following words of truth, which I saw in the Holy Trinity while I was rapt in prayer, to those blessed brothers who hold office. Whenever a person prays in Christian faith with such a humble heart that they cannot bear any creature beneath them and with such a rapt soul that everything must fall away from them in their prayer except God alone, then they are a divine god with the heavenly Father.[125] But yet, that is the very best time to remember how pitiful they are in themselves; they are so fearful of themselves in the sweet embrace that their only concern is God's honour. However, when a person works for a just cause through real need with the same love with which they have prayed, then they are a human god with Christ. But all that which we mess around with aimlessly and purposelessly is dead in the eyes of God.

But when a person, for love of God and not for earthly reward, teaches the ignorant and converts the sinner and comforts the distressed and brings the desperate back to God, then they are a spiritual god with the Holy Spirit.

Ah, that person is greatly blessed who does all things that are praiseworthy to God, and within the grasp of mankind, with the same degree of love and with the constant will of their whole heart to honour God, for they are then a complete person with the Holy Trinity. But the dust of sin that falls on us even against our will is quickly burnt off by the fire of love as the glance of the eyes of the soul touches the Godhead in painful, sighing and sweet desire that no creature may withstand. When she begins to ascend, then the dust of sin falls away from her, and so she becomes a goddess with God, so that what He wants, she wants too and only in this way can they be united in complete union.

Ah, my friend, you should devote a free hour every day or every night to Our dear Lord God, in which, undisturbed, you can pray lovingly, for the heavenly gift, with which God is accustomed to greet and teach his chosen dear ones, is by nature so noble and so fine and flows so sweetly when the eternal God wants to go to the eager Soul in the narrow bridal bed;[126] He is so wounded by her love that He renounced all things that were pleasurable to Him for more than thirty years so that He might cover her with kisses and embrace her with His bare arms. If you would remember this, how could you

---

[125] Cf. p. 53, n. 53.
[126] Cf. p. 30, n. 7.

be so boorish as not to give Him one hour a day in return for thirty years.

When I, most wretched of all people, go to pray, then I attire myself in keeping with my unworthiness, and so I clothe myself with the mire[127] that I am. Then I pull on the shoes of the noble time that I have lost every day; and then I gird myself with the pain that I have deserved. After that I put on a cloak of wickedness, of which I am full; then I set upon my head a crown of the secret disgrace I have incurred before God. After that I take in my hand a mirror of true knowledge; in it I see who I really am. Then, unfortunately, I see nothing but woe and more woe. I prefer to wear these clothes rather than all the earthly splendour that I could wish for, and at the same time they cause me such distress in my wretched impatience that I would rather be clothed with Hell and crowned with all the devils through no fault of my own. Alas, how often, unfortunately, do the robbers of inconstancy come and take these clothes from us; when we please ourselves and we claim to be guiltless in our guilt, then we are robbed by vain honour and struck down by arrogance and then we are more naked than naked. Alas, how great our shame must then be before God and before His friends and before all creatures.

If we would overcome our shame with great honour, then we must clothe ourselves again with ourselves. Thus attired, I seek Jesus my sweet Lord and I never find Him so fast as with that which is offensive and painful. We should go to Him bravely, with powerful desire and with guilty shame and with flowing love and with humble fear, for then the filth of sin disappears before the divine eyes of Our Lord; and so He begins to shine lovingly towards the Soul and she begins to flow with heartfelt love; there the Soul sheds all her guilt and all her sorrow; and as He begins to teach her all His will, so she begins to taste His sweetness; and then He begins to greet her with His Godhead so that the force of the Holy Trinity penetrates her soul and her body,[128] and so she receives true wisdom; and then He begins to caress her so that she becomes weak, then she begins to drink deeply so that He becomes lovesick; and then He begins to temper the measure, for He knows the Soul's capacity better than she knows it

---

[127] Cf. p. 40, n. 23.

[128] There is a blurring of the focus here. Where just before Mechthild had been talking about the Soul, she seems here to be talking of the whole person, referring to the person's soul and body. A few lines further on Mechthild reverts to talking about the 'Soul', but shortly afterwards she once more refers to the person's 'flesh' and 'soul'.

herself, and then she begins to want to demonstrate great faith to Him; and so He begins to give her full knowledge, and then, joyfully, she begins to feel His love on her flesh; and then He begins to strengthen in her soul all His gifts with holy feeling. If she can then protect herself from the base love of her flesh and from the acquisitive sweetness of all earthly things, then she may love perfectly and win much praise for God in all things.

Now, my friend, there are two further things which you should protect yourself from with holy diligence, for they never bore holy fruit: The first is the man or woman who dedicates themselves to good deeds and good conduct only so that they might be chosen for high office; this is inimical to my soul. When these people seize hold of power, their vices become so manifold that there is no one who had chosen them with great eagerness who receives comfort from them. They are then led astray by honours and their false virtues are turned to vices. The second is the person who is chosen without any of their own doing but then changes so much that they never wish to relinquish office; this is a sign of much vice. Even if they conduct themselves in a praiseworthy way, they should nonetheless always be fearful and humble themselves.

That honest woman and worthy man who would speak with me, but after my death cannot, should read this little book.

VI, 2. Of the rule of a canon; how he should conduct himself. This has come from God

We should greet people in the Holy Spirit with His divine succour, and we should give thanks for their merciful gifts. But even more, we should give thanks together with all creatures to the Heavenly Father for the holy gift that He pours forth unceasingly from his Holy Trinity into the hearts of sinners day after day. It is no thanks to the owl that the eagle soars so high.[129]

I prayed on behalf of a clergyman at his request.[130] This is the holy response from God and this is what He says to me: 'It is his wish to sink into a humble life and the gift I give him is great and his will is holy; but he should remain just where he is.' God, the supreme pope

---

[129] Neumann (1993: 112) notes that the introductory paragraph of this chapter has nothing to do with what follows and is not present in the corresponding chapter in the *Ld*. It would seem that it has been added, for whatever reason, at a later stage. The final sentence of this paragraph sounds as if it is derived from a proverb.

[130] This man is identified in the *Ld* (519, 8) as 'Dietrich, the venerable deacon of the church of Magdeburg'.

of Heaven, has sent him this rule and says: 'He should always pray constantly according to priestly ordinance. In addition, I will give him my divine sweetness; this he should enjoy in the solitude of his heart. Whenever he is tempted, he should call out to me with might and main and I shall rush to his help. He should pay his debts in full and incur little expense. He should have no one in his service either by virtue of his position or through extravagance; but he should have honest servants to attend to his real needs. He should not concern himself with his relatives; but he should help any of them who wish to follow him.[131] He should wear good clothes, as he does now; but next to his skin he should wear clothes of rough material to offset the many tactile pleasures he has had. He should also sleep on straw between two woollen blankets, and he should have two pillows under his head,[132] and during the day he should cover his bed with a beautiful quilt, and his bed shall stand in the same place where it has always been, visible to all. In front of his bed there shall be a mat and a prayer stool. In this way, with a humble heart, he should set a good example to those living an unworthy life. He shall also have two scourges by his bed with which he will mortify his flesh when he awakes.

Once every day he shall pray, fully prostrated, as follows: 'Lord, Heavenly Father, God of Heaven, I, an unworthy person, thank You, Lord, for having bestowed Your grace on me. Now I beseech You, dearest Father, with all Your friends, that the sweet, heavenly flood, which pours down here unceasingly from the overflowing, living fountain[133] of Your complete Holy Trinity, might always cleanse my soul of all stains. *Per dominum nostrum.*'[134]

After this I asked: 'How shall he keep himself free of sin in earthly honour?' Then Our Lord said: 'He should keep himself in a state of constant fear just like a mouse that sits in the trap, awaiting its death.

---

[131]   That is, into the priesthood.

[132]   Cf. IV, 27 (p. 82).

[133]   Cf. Mechthild's frequent use of the image of the Holy Trinity as a fountain in Book I: I, 2 (p. 27); I, 4 (p. 29); I, 22 (p. 30); I, 44 (p. 35).

[134]   'Through Our Lord'. Although Mechthild draws attention to her ignorance of Latin (e.g., II, 3, 48), she would have been familiar with the Latin of the liturgy, the Psalter and the daily canonical hours. She occasionally inserts a phrase in Latin, usually liturgical or biblical in origin, into her writings. Of the thirty-four incidences of such quotations, it is interesting that twenty-one of them are to be found in Books VI and VII. This concentration probably reflects her association with the highly educated nuns of Helfta while she was writing these books. Cf. Margetts (1977: 126, n. 14).

The lowest part of the trap is earthly honour; the uppermost part is my almighty power.' The Lord glosses this as follows: 'Whoever would enjoy my true taste must at all times and in all things have a dread of the body's taste in which the heart delights with secret pleasure. Therefore, when he eats he should be modest and generous;[135] when he sleeps he should be disciplined and alone with me. When he is in company he should be a mouse in his heart; when he makes his confession he should be truthful and obedient and should do all that is required of him by his confessor.'

VI, 3. God gives authority. How the goats become lambs

It is God's will that this same clergyman has been chosen to be deacon,[136] for God Himself has spoken thus: 'I have moved him from one chair to another so that he might provide nourishment for the goats.' The gloss: The reason that God calls the cathedral clergy goats is because their flesh stinks of incontinence in the eternal truth of his Holy Trinity. The goat's skin is noble and so it is with their spiritual authority and their prebend; but when this skin is shed at death then they lose all their nobility. And Our Lord God was asked in what way these goats might become lambs. Then Our Lord spoke thus: 'If they will eat the fodder that Canon Dietrich lays in the manger for them, that is, holy penance and faithful counsel in confession, then they will become the kind of lambs one calls rams, lambs with horns.' The horn represents spiritual power, which they make use of in a holy fashion to the honour of God. We should be strong and have complete faith in God, for He says: 'I myself shall help with the successful expiation of these men's guilt.'

VI, 7. Our self-will can withstand Barb. The good Soul is quickly with God

In my community there is a religious person who causes me much distress because of her bad behaviour, for this person will not obey me in anything.[137] I complained to God about this and wanted to know why this should be the case. Then Our Lord said: 'See what is causing this trouble.' Then I saw that a special devil had attached

---

[135] That is, modest where his own needs are concerned and generous towards others.

[136] There is a marginal gloss in Latin in Ms E that says 'About the aforementioned canon of Magdeburg'. Cf. Ancelet-Hustache (1926: 203f.) on the historical figure of Dietrich.

[137] This remark has led to the supposition that Mechthild acted as the *magistra* in a beguine convent in Magdeburg. Cf. Grundmann (1935/77: 328).

himself to this person and was holding her back from all good things. Then I said: 'Who has given you the power to treat God with such contempt in this person?' Then the devil said: 'No one save only her own self-will has given me this power.' In these words I saw that the devil, with great contemptuous scorn, followed all religious people who allow him access to themselves by living such false lives and protesting their innocence before God and all creatures. Then I said; 'Who should help this person to be freed of you?' Then the devil, compelled by God, said: 'No one can help her but her own self-will, for God has given her the power to change her attitude. If she does that, then I shall have to hurry away from her.' 'Now, I ask you in eternal truth: What is your name?' Then the devil said: 'I am called Barb and the crowd which you see back there are all my pals, doing the same job as myself, and there are as many of them as there are of people who are not willing to obey their faithful superiors in good things.'

At this my soul turned so swiftly to God that she soared without any effort and snuggled herself right into the Holy Trinity as a child snuggles into its mother's coat and rests itself right on her breast. Then my Soul spoke thus with the power and the voice of all creatures: 'Ah dear Love, now consider the distress this person causes me and, Lord, change her attitude with Your divine sweetness.' 'No,' said Our Lord, 'she is not worthy of my sweetness, but I will afflict her body with a sickness that will make her lame from the pain so that she will not walk along sinful paths, and I shall strike her dumb so that she shall not utter bad words. She shall also become so blind that she is ashamed to look at vain things. But whatever is then done for her is done for me.' And indeed this happened fourteen days later. Alleluia.

VI, 15. Of the torment of Enoch and Elijah[138] and of the last preachers and of the wickedness of the Antichrist

O powerful Love divine, you have afflicted me with such sweet distress that my soul is consumed by the desire for wonder. When I consider that death shall snuff out my body so that I shall no longer be able to suffer for, nor praise my dear Jesus, then I am in such distress that, were it possible, I would like to survive until the Day of Judgement; faithful Love, which is God's alone and not mine, drives me to this. On this matter Our Lord said: 'If you are about to die, then

---

[138] Cf. IV, 27; VII, 57.

repent all your days, however holy you might be.' 'Ah, Lord, I beg of You that my desire may not die when I can no longer do anything with my body.' Then Our Lord said: 'Your desire shall live, for it cannot die because it is eternal. If it thus waits for me until the end of time, then Soul and Body will be reunited; when I shall return the Soul to the Body, she will praise me for evermore. And she has served me from the very beginning, because you have wanted to be with Adam until now for the sake of my love; in this way you wished to embrace all human suffering and all human service for my sake; I tell you further: Your being shall continue to exist until the last person on earth.'

'Ah, my very dear Love, who shall be the last person with whom my being shall associate, for there shall be precious few religious people alive at the end of the world?' Our Lord answered thus: 'Enoch shall be the last person who shall practise a religious life.'[139]

After that God showed me the end of the world once again,[140] when the last brothers shall suffer martyrdom as follows. In accordance with a particular provision of God's will, their hair should never be cut; the Antichrist orders them to be hung by it from a tree. They shall hang there and die a noble death, for within them their hearts burn with the sweet fire of Heaven in the same measure that their bodies suffer in torment. Therefore, their souls, without any dread of this pain, part from their bodies between the comfort of the Holy Spirit and the suffering of the wretched flesh. Elijah and Enoch shall travel from India to the sea and both of them shall be followed by a large crowd, all of whom are Christians flocking to them from the Antichrist. They are all slain, just like mad dogs that have been fatally poisoned and are hunted down in the street. But then others follow them who are secret Christians, because God has made them fully aware that that is the only way they can escape unbelief.

Elijah will be the first to be martyred and he shall be bound and nailed by his hands to a high cross. They do this out of fierce hatred because he was forever speaking of the holy cross and what happened to Christ on it. They do not allow him to die, so that he might suffer a long time and might recant Christian teaching and thus turn to the Antichrist. And so the beloved of holy God hangs there and gives no voice to his suffering. He comforts holy Christianity for

---

[139] Cf. Genesis 5: 21–24; Hebrews 11: 5 and, in the Apocrypha, Ecclesiasticus (Sirach) 44: 16.
[140] Cf. IV, 27.

three days and nights until his soul departs. I saw the heavenly Father at his end and He received the soul of Elijah with His human hands and said:[141] 'Come, my dear one, it is time.' And in a flash of heavenly light God took him away. That accursed person Antichrist does not allow the burial of God's beloved because he wishes all Christians to recant. In this he is mistaken, for all who look on the body are moved to Christian faith, and it gives them joy to pray to it, for they become so filled with the sweetness of the presence of the holy body that they forget the pain of death and all earthly riches.

Enoch, however, is still alive, for it pleases the Antichrist to hear all the wisdom that Enoch has learnt from God, so that he might pervert it publicly with his false teaching and were he able to draw Enoch to him, then all the world would be his with great honour.

In the meantime, so many of the wicked are drawn away from the Antichrist that he attacks Enoch with furious words and only then does Enoch tell the Antichrist the whole truth (as follows): 'You are a scourge for the world, sent by God because of the evil of the wicked and the holiness of the good. You are as familiar with the scriptures of the Old Testament as you are with those of the New; now see what your deeds will bring you to. In this you have made your choice eagerly: according to Scripture you shall be lost; you can read that for yourself. You have created neither the Earth nor Heaven, you do not give the angels eternal life, you have not made the soul and body of mankind, you have never given a creature natural life. How then could you be God? All your deeds are accomplished through lying in false cunning. Jesus Christ, who is an eternal God with His Father, is the eternal truth.'

Then the Antichrist speaks with fury: 'How dare you name my enemy in my presence, in whom you recognise greater honour than in myself? I will have satisfaction from you and I will rid all the world of you. By my power, take hold of him quickly and pour boiling pitch into his mouth and strangle him, then my enemy will be silent. If I wanted to hear his words I would happily let him suffer longer. Then hang him up dead, high above all the murderers, so that everyone who sees him might abandon the Christian faith. He has attacked my honour; no one needs his teaching. I have long been anticipated, things will happen in accordance with my teaching.'

Enoch says his holy prayer in his pure heart: 'Eternal Father and

---

[141] In the account of this vision Mechthild moves between the present and the past tense.

Son and Holy Spirit, You eternal God indivisible, I thank You, Lord, for having chosen me long ago and I praise You now, Lord, in this torment. I pray to You, Lord, for Your sheep and mine that are now left without a shepherd; protect each one of them and comfort them secretly. Now receive, Lord, my soul; I have no earthly love for my body.' The answer that God will make him for his thanksgiving and his prayer is written here. I saw it and read it written in the Holy Trinity (as follows): 'Dear son, now come to me quickly, I am truly in you. Your friends, for whom you have prayed to me, shall baptise their children themselves; I shall free them quickly from the Antichrist. They shall remain Christians in their hearts and I shall protect them from all despair. Come, dear friend. I am waiting for you and my heart leaps forward to meet you.'

VI, 21. How the unworthy priesthood should be humbled; [how only preachers should preach and be bishops] and of the last brothers[142]

Alas, Crown of Holy Christendom, how greatly you have been desecrated! You have lost your precious stones because you are damaging and defiling the holy Christian faith; your gold is tarnished in the mire[143] of incontinence, for you have been beggared and do not have true love; your chastity has been consumed in the greedy fire of appetite; your humility is sunk in the quagmire of your flesh; your truth has become void in the lies of this world; the flowers of all your virtues have dropped from you.

Alas, Crown of the Holy Priesthood, how you have faded! Indeed, you have nothing left but the trappings of your office, that is, priestly authority with which you fight against God and His chosen friends. For this God shall humble you before you know it, for Our Lord speaks thus: 'I shall touch the heart of the Pope in Rome with great sorrow and I shall speak to him in this sorrow and complain to him that my shepherds of Jerusalem have become murderers and wolves, because they murder the white lambs before my eyes; and that the old sheep are all addled, because they cannot graze on the healthy pasture of divine love and holy teaching which grows in the high mountains.

Whoever knows nothing of the path to Hell, let him observe the

---

[142] Neumann (1993: 125) doubts whether the phrase in brackets is authentic and points to the probable influence of the teachings of Joachim of Fiore on Mechthild's conception of 'the last brothers'.

[143] Cf. p. 40, n. 23.

depraved priesthood, how their lives with women and with children and with other manifest sins lead them directly to Hell. That is why it is time for the last brothers to come; for the cloak that is old is also cold. And so I must give my Bride, Holy Christianity, a new cloak.' This shall be the last brothers about whom I have written before.[144]

'Pope, my son, if you make this happen, then you will prolong your life; the reason that your predecessors did not live long is because they did not execute my hidden will.' Thus I saw the pope in prayer and then I heard God communicating this to him.

VI, 23. How God speaks to the Soul in three places
The Devil often speaks to the Soul in the first place. He cannot in the other two. The first place is a person's senses. This place is equally open to God, the Devil and all creatures and there they may speak as they will. The second place, where God speaks to the Soul, is in the Soul. No one other than God may enter this place. When God, however, speaks in the Soul, that happens, without any kind of awareness on the part of the Senses, in a great, powerful, swift union of God with the Soul; and so the Senses cannot hear the blissful communication. They become so humble that they cannot bear any creature beneath them. Should a person humble themselves beneath the Devil?[145] Yes, with the intention of realising that they have shown God such great contempt in the way they have lived in that they have often drawn the Devil's likeness on their soul with venial sins and have, from time to time, cut deep into their soul with mortal sins. The Soul that is embraced by the Holy Spirit cannot restrain herself from sinking away from all earthly comfort and from delight in this comfort. But the Soul that is caught up in her own self-will inclines with much delight to earthly things. The third place where God speaks to the Soul is in Heaven, when God transports the Soul in the delight of His will and holds her there where she may delight in His wonder.

---

[144] Cf. IV, 27.
[145] Cf. V, 4 (p. 88).

VI, 31. How God made the Soul; of pleasure and suffering; how God is like a sphere[146]

I said in a passage in this book that the Godhead is my Father by nature.[147] You did not understand this and you said: 'Everything that God has done with us is through grace, not through nature.' 'You are right and I am right too. Now listen to an analogy: however wonderful a person's eyes are, they cannot see over a mile away. However acute a person's senses are, they cannot grasp abstract things except through faith and they grope in the darkness like a blind person. The loving Soul, that loves everything that God loves and hates everything that God hates, has an eye that God has illumined; with it she sees into the eternal Godhead, how the Godhead has worked with His nature in the Soul. He has fashioned her in His own image; He has planted her in Himself; of all creatures He has united Himself most fully with her; He has enclosed her in Himself and has poured so much of His divine nature into her that she cannot say other than that in all this union He is more than her Father.'

The Body has its dignity from the Son of the Heavenly Father in brotherly fellowship and in the reward for its work. The Son of God, Jesus Christ, also performed His work in heartfelt love through need in poverty, in suffering through effort, in humiliation until His holy death. The Holy Spirit has also performed His work, as you say, through His grace and all the gifts we have ever received.

These works are of three kinds and yet one undivided God has performed them in us. Two things are constantly at work on Earth and in Purgatory through the power of God. One of these things works only in Heaven, another works only in Hell: that is, pleasure in Heaven without suffering and suffering in Hell without pleasure.

Where was God before He created anything? He was in Himself and all things were present and visible to Him as they are today. What shape did Our Lord God have then? Just exactly like a sphere and all things were enclosed within God without lock or door. The lowest part of the sphere is a bottomless foundation beneath all abysses, the uppermost part is a height beyond which there is no other, the

---

[146] On the Neo-Platonic origins and dissemination of the exegetical image of God as a circle and a sphere, see Ruh (1993: 276f.), Neumann (1993: 132f.) and Schmidt (1995: 393f.). McGinn (1998: 234) draws attention to the 'unusually scholastic-sounding' tone of this passage.

[147] Mechthild is defending a comment made in an earlier passage (I, 44 [p. 36]) which appears to have aroused some scepticism.

circumference of the sphere is an incomprehensible circle. At this time, God had not yet become Creator. However, when He did create all things, was the sphere then opened up? No, it remained intact and it shall always remain intact. When God became Creator all creation became manifest: mankind to love God, to delight in God and to know Him, and to remain obedient to Him; birds and animals to be true to their nature; inanimate creation to stand as it is. Now listen: What we know is all nothing, unless we love God properly in all things, as He Himself has created all things in proper love and has offered and taught us love.

VI, 35. How the Soul that is blessed speaks to the Body on the Day of Judgement

Rise up, my beloved, and be restored after all your suffering, all your days of sorrow, all your humiliation, all your sadness, all your loneliness, all your pain and all your travail. The morning star has risen with the birth and life of St Mary. The sun has shone brightly; that is, God became man, toiled and ascended into Heaven. The moon shall always stand fast; that is, we shall stand fast in life eternal. At one time all my salvation rested with you, now all your consolation rests with me. Had I not returned to you, you would never have been raised from these ashes. Eternal day has dawned for us; now we shall receive our reward.

VI, 36. That John the Baptist sang a mass for the poor maid was spiritual knowledge in the Soul[148]

We cannot comprehend divine gifts with human senses. That is why people, whose spirit is not open to the invisible truth, sin against themselves. That which we can see with the eyes of the Body, can hear with the ears of the Body, can speak with the mouth of the Body, that is as unlike the truth revealed to the loving Soul as a wax candle is to the bright sun. That John the Baptist sang Mass for the poor maid was not a physical reality; it was a spiritual experience that only the Soul saw, understood and delighted in. But the Body had nothing of this except what it could comprehend in its human senses through the nobility of the Soul; that is why the words must be couched in human terms.

In response to this account my Pharisee said that John the Baptist

---

[148]   This chapter is a response to criticism of an earlier vision of John the Baptist celebrating Mass (II, 4).

was a layman. The most sacred thing in the Mass is the Body of God. John the Baptist touched the Son of this same God with humble, trembling fear; his holy life was so greatly distinguished that he heard the voice of the heavenly Father and understood His words and saw the Holy Spirit and knew the Son in them both. John the Baptist also preached the holy Christian faith publicly to everyone and, with his finger, pointed out to the people the true Son of God, who was present: 'Ecce agnus dei.'[149] Never will a pope or bishop or priest be able to speak the Word of God as John the Baptist did; they can only do this with our supernatural Christian faith. Was this man a layman? Answer me this, o you blind; your lies and your hate will never be forgiven you without punishment.

VI, 38. No one can destroy God's Heaven. Hell drives away God

'Ah, dear Lord, almighty God, how long must I remain here in this earthly flesh like a stake, or a target at which people run, throw and shoot and who have assailed my honour with swift malice for a long time?' Now hear this answer: 'No one is so fleet of foot, no one can throw so powerfully, no one can shoot with such cunning, no one is so malicious in their fury that they might destroy or wreck or cause damage to my Heaven in which I dwell. Furthermore: the place where I am offered refuge today and thrown out tomorrow resembles Hell. Where I am the foundation, I shall also be the pinnacle.' 'Ah, Lord, who shall help me to walk along all my paths so that, should I slip, I will not fall?' The fear of God shall hold me upright, the will of God shall lead me.

VI, 41. Of the reflection of God in mankind and in the angels. Five things inhibit writing

You want me to carry on writing and I cannot. The bliss, the glory, the brightness, the loving embrace, the truth, this is so overwhelming that I fell silent, unable to speak any more about what I know.

But yet: In the Kingdom of Heaven a mirror[150] was seen in front of the breast of each and every soul [and body]. In it the mirror of the Holy Trinity shines, giving truth and knowledge of all those virtues which the Body ever practised and all the gifts which the Soul ever received on Earth. From here the noble reflection of each person

---

[149] 'Behold the Lamb of God' (John 1: 29).
[150] Cf. p. 29, n. 6.

shines back into the sublime Majesty from which they have flowed. The reflection of the angels is fiery bright in love, for our well being is very dear to them. They serve us without effort and their reward grows as long as the world exists. The true love of God has the same power in mankind as it has in the angels. That we serve with effort is because we are sinful.

Book VII

Book VII opens on an apocalyptic note with a detailed account of the crown, seen with the eyes of the soul, that symbolically represents all those who shall enjoy the Kingdom of Heaven after the Day of Judgement (VII, 1). Mechthild's preoccupation with the afterlife finds further expression in the account of the passage of the individual loving soul into Heaven and the consequent frustration of the inmates of Hell (VII, 39).

In this final book Mechthild reflects on the passage of time (VII, 3) and the physical impact it has had on her (VII, 64), although she is still capable of forgetting her infirmity when Christ appears to her as a young man (VII, 8). In a personal meditation on the penitential psalms (VII, 35), Mechthild describes the gamut of her various relationships with God, highlighting once more the pre-eminent role of the Bride. There is a resurgence of the passionate nature of her love for God (VII, 8; VII, 58; VII, 59) that was expressed so memorably in Books I and II.

Book VII was written in the convent at Helfta. Attention is drawn to this context in Mechthild's anxiety about her function in the community (VII, 8). Even though she receives assurance from God that she is among kindred spirits (VII, 14), she nonetheless feels compelled to express her sense of inferiority and unworthiness, once more, as an 'ignorant' woman amongst the learned nuns (VII, 21). That Mechthild was held in high regard by the nuns is suggested, however, by their desire for her teaching (VII, 21), and their bidding her to intercede with God about the local wars in Saxony and Thuringia (VII, 10; VII, 28). Mechthild expresses a more positive sense of the community around her both in her thanks for the physical support she is given (VII, 64) and in her spiritual allegory of the convent (VII, 36).

Further visions of Purgatory (VII, 41), the Apocalypse (VII, 57) and the Nativity (VII, 60) are recorded, the three subjects that feature most frequently in Mechthild's visionary life. The work is brought to a harmonious conclusion (VII, 65) in the resolution of that conflict between the Body and the Soul that had emerged right at the outset (I, 2). Mechthild's final words are on the paramount importance of obedience, that aspect of the religious life that she had constantly highlighted through her abiding concern with the prevalence of destructive self-will.

VII, 1. Of the crown and of the honour which Our Lord Jesus Christ shall receive after the Day of Judgement

Our Lord, heavenly Father, has in His divine wisdom kept back many indescribable gifts, with which, after the Day of Judgement, He will adorn His elect children: In particular, the heavenly Father has ready for His only begotten Son Jesus, Our Redeemer, a crown, which has been wrought and adorned with such great, wonderful and varied art that all the masters that ever were and now are and ever shall be could never completely describe the brightness and the manifold splendour of this crown. This crown was seen with the spiritual eyes of the loving Soul in everlasting eternity and its nature was apprehended. What is this thing eternity? It is the uncreated wisdom of the infinite Godhead that has neither beginning nor end.

The crown has three arches: the first arch was that of the patriarchs, the second that of the prophets, the third that of holy Christianity. The crown was fashioned and graced with the presence of all the blessed, who on the Day of Judgement shall possess the kingdom of God; they shall, however, be honoured in accordance with their deeds.

The first arch of the crown is worked in gold and illuminated with the precious stones of holy fervour and all the good deeds ever performed by the patriarchs. This arch is also fashioned with the image, soul and body of mankind. The first image on the arch of the crown is Saint Stephen and all those martyrs whose blood has been spilt for the Christian faith are depicted with him. Saint Peter is also depicted together with all God's Apostles and all those blessed who followed the teachings of the Apostles. Those married people, who have followed God with good deeds, shall also be depicted, together with their children, on this arch.

The second arch of the crown is fashioned with all the popes and with them all the spiritual fraternity, into whose care God entrusted His sheep. This arch is worked in spiritual authority and adorned with the flowers of Christian teaching.

The third arch of the crown is fashioned most beautifully with the noble humanity of our Lord Jesus Christ and with Him His glorious mother Mary with all her virgins, who shall follow the Lamb. Saint John the Baptist is portrayed very close to the Lamb and with him all those who became Christians at his hands. This arch of the crown is worked with the creation of all creatures in that spirit of love and intention with which the Creator created everything according to His will.

The crown is adorned all over with many chivalric shields of holy, mighty Christian faith. The empire shall also be depicted on the crown, fashioned and adorned with every last peasant, always in accordance with how well they served God.

The crown shall also be crenulated at the time of the Antichrist with many a fine picture, such as that of Elijah and Enoch, and many holy martyrs before them will be adorned with the sanctity of their lives and glorified through their precious blood.

The crown shall also be stained with the blood of the Lamb and illuminated and gilded with that powerful love which broke the sweet heart of Jesus. Our heavenly Father has created this crown, Jesus Christ has earned it, the Holy Spirit has wrought it and forged it in fiery love and has made it so fitting through the noble art of the Holy Trinity that it suits our Redeemer Jesus Christ so well and looks so magnificent on Him that the heavenly Father receives yet more delight from His only begotten Son. That must be, for even though the eternal Godhead without beginning had, now has, and ever shall have, all pleasure and joy within Himself, nonetheless it gives Him particular eternal pleasure that He may contemplate with such joy His eternal Son and all those who follow Him.

As soon as Jesus Christ has delivered His last judgement and has served at and celebrated His supper, He shall receive in great honour this crown from His heavenly Father and with Him those who have, through service, come to the eternal feast with body and soul. Then each soul and body shall see their honour in the crown.

The crown is created on earth at great cost, not with silver, nor with gold, nor with precious stones, but with human effort, with human tears, sweat and blood, with all virtue and in the final resort with painful death. The angels do not appear on the crown as they are not people. However, they must praise God for the crown with glorious song.

The first choir sings thus: 'We praise You, Lord, for Your glorious Testament, for all those represented on the crown come from this.' The second choir: 'We praise You, Lord, with the faith of Abraham and with the ardent desire and prophecies of all prophets.' The third choir: 'We praise You, Lord, with the wisdom and devotion of all Your Apostles.' The fourth choir: 'We praise You, Lord, with the blood and with the patience of all Your martyrs.' The fifth choir: 'We praise You, Lord, for the holy prayer and Christian teaching of all baptists and confessors.' The sixth choir: 'We praise You, Lord, with the constant penitence of Your widows.' The seventh choir: 'We praise You, Lord, with the chastity of all virgins.' The eighth choir: 'We praise You, Lord, with the fruit of Your holy Virgin Mother.' The ninth choir: 'We praise You, Lord, for Your holy death and for Your glorious life after Your death and for Your great outpouring of all gifts and all goodness, with which You have raised us up and ordered us with honour; we praise You, Lord, with Your fiery love within which You have united us.'

Up above the crown flies the most beautiful standard that was ever seen in this empire; this shall be the holy cross, on which Christ suffered His death. The cross has four points. The lowest point is adorned with joy brighter than the sun. At the point on the right, under the cross, is suspended upright the wooden stave, stained with the blood of the Lamb, decorated and adorned with the nails with which Our Lord was wounded. At the top of the tree of the cross hangs the imperial Crown of Thorns – most glorious and royal. The thorns are coloured lily white, rose pink, and are joyful and bright as Heaven. This is the standard of the crown, with which Jesus Christ won the victory and returned living to His Father.

At the eternal celebration, immediately after the Day of Judgement, when God will have made everything new, this crown shall be revealed and shall rest on the head of the humanity of Our Lord, to the honour and praise of the Holy Trinity and to the joy of all the blessed for ever more.

The humanity of Our Lord is an intelligible image of His eternal divinity, so that we may comprehend the Godhead with our humanity, and, like the Holy Trinity, delight in, hug and kiss and embrace incomprehensible God, Whom neither Heaven nor Earth, Hell nor Purgatory can ever grasp or resist. The eternal Godhead shines and radiates and makes all the blessed in His presence eager for love so that, free from toil, they rejoice and shall always live free of suffering. The humanity of Our Lord greets, delights in and loves unceasingly His flesh and blood. For even though flesh and blood are now no more, the fraternal kinship is nonetheless so great that He must love His human nature specially.

The Holy Spirit also gives from His loving heavenly outpouring, with which He fills the cup of the blessed and gives them so much to drink that they sing with joy, laugh sweetly and spring gracefully and flow and swim; they fly and climb from choir to choir to the pinnacle of Heaven, where they look into the mirror of eternity and know the will and all the works of the Holy Trinity and how they themselves have been shaped in body and soul as they shall remain for ever-more.[151] The Soul is fashioned in the Body in the likeness of man and has the divine radiance within her and shines through the Body as lustrous gold does through clear crystal.

And so they become so joyful and so free, quick, powerful and rich in love, clear and as like God as they can be. And so they go wherever they wish, covering a thousand miles in the time that it takes to think a thought; imagine what this movement is like! And yet they can never touch nor grasp the end of this kingdom. The broad expanse of space and the golden streets are so enormous and yet quite in proportion and in fact not golden because they are eternally more valuable than gold and precious stones; the latter are all of this Earth and shall be destroyed.

And now we come to the end of the crown: the Holy Spirit shall continue to fashion this crown until the Day of Judgement. Then the Father and the Son shall reward Him for His work. God will give Him as a reward all the souls and bodies that are gathered together in His kingdom; the Holy Spirit shall rest within them for all eternity and He shall greet them and delight them unceasingly. Everything that was ever good because of God's love or ever will be, everything that was suffered and abandoned for God, all that must form part of the ornament of the crown. Ah, what a crown! Ah, who will help me so that I might yet be a tiny little flower on the crown, like the baptised infants who are the tiniest flowers on it?

If this piece is too long it is because I have found so much pleasure in the crown. And yet I have compressed so much into so few words. This is what I say to myself: 'For how long are you going to keep on barking, wretched whelp? You must shut up, for I must be silent about that which is most precious.'

VII, 3. How valuable it is for a person to examine their heart constantly with humble fear

I know of no one so good that they have no need to examine their heart constantly, to acknowledge what they find there and also to find fault regularly with all they do. This one should do with humble fear. God's voice taught me this, for I never did anything so well that I could not have done it better. This is my reproach to myself.

Now this is how we should take our frailty to task: 'Oh you most

---

[151] There is a concentration here of recurrent images, particularly in the first three books.

wretched creature, how long will you harbour useless habits in your five senses? Our childhood was foolish, our youth was challenged; God knows how successful we have been in this. Oh alas, my age is now the object of my reproach because it is not capable of shining deeds and, unfortunately, it is cold in grace. It is also powerless since it does not have youth to cope with the fiery love of God. It is also greatly bothered by minor ailments, which youth pays little attention to. And yet good old age is happily forbearing and trusts in God alone.

Seven years ago a distressed old person[152] complained about this impairment to Our Lord. Then God answered her thus: 'Your childhood was a companion to my Holy Spirit; your youth was a bride to my Humanity; your old age is now a wife to my Godhead.'

Alas, dear Lord! What use is it that the dog barks? If the master is asleep, the thief will break into his house. But sometimes the prayer of the pure heart does rouse the dead sinner. O sinner! How much cause you may give us to weep, for you are your own murderer and you are a threat to all goodness and yet also a benefit to it. The good person derives great benefit from seeing how someone else is presumptuous or falls into sin, for then they are very circumspect, so that they may not land in the same trouble; in this way the good person improves themselves through bad things; then good works follow willingly close behind; but the bad person becomes worse, for when they see bad examples they become so bad that they scorn good deeds and good people. Their own perverted wisdom pleases them best.

My dear Schoolmaster, who instructed me, a simple and stupid woman, in this book, also taught me the following: you should not be intimate with the person who does not act with integrity, whatever they might do. I know an enemy who erases divine truth in the human heart. If he is allowed in, then, with the consent of the person, he will inscribe his false truth in their heart saying: 'It is my nature to be angry and weak.' You cannot use this to excuse yourself before God or for the sake of your honour. Through grace you should become meek and strong.

'I have no grace.' Then you should call upon gracious God in your lack of grace with humble tears and with constant prayer in holy desire. In this way the worm of anger shall die. You should be hard on yourself so that there will be no need for God or anyone else to inflict

152 Cf. p. 76, n. 83.

pain on you. In this way the worm of anger will be crushed. If we wish to overcome and drive out our anger and all our imperfection through God, then, privately, we simply have to ignore our sinful temptations and, outwardly, conduct ourselves with a holy, joyful demeanour.

Alas, wretches! No matter how long we rage in anger, we must nonetheless, if there is any good in us, keep returning to our heart; then we shall have reason to be ashamed of ourselves; anger has consumed our power and has dried up our flesh and so we have wasted our precious time in which we should have been serving God. Alas, that is an eternal shame! And alas, again! I feel remorse for the sinful tears that are wept in arrogant anger. The soul becomes so darkened by them that for a while the person is incapable of making good use of anything. The tears of remorse are so holy: if a great sinner were to weep a tear of remorse for each of their sins and remain in this state of mind, they would never go to eternal Hell.

However trivial the venial sins that a good person is guilty of and refuses to rid himself of while they are alive, if they die without confession and penance, they must go to bitter Purgatory, no matter how holy they are. For as merciful as God is, He is also just and hostile to all sins. I tell myself that love must always be with us; we should never be self-righteous. Then humility will dwell within!

VII, 8. How a person might seek God

When God wants to be distant from a person,[153] then she looks for Our Lord God and says: 'Lord, my suffering is deeper than the abyss, the sorrow of my heart is wider than the world, my fear is taller than the mountains, my longing is higher than the stars; I cannot find You anywhere in these things.' In the midst of this distress the Soul became aware of her Love, in the shape of a young man of ineffable beauty; and yet she would have hidden herself. However, she falls to His feet and kisses His wounds; they are so sweet that she completely forgets her pain and her age. Then she thought: 'Alas, how much you would like to see His face, but you would have to forego His wounds, and how much you would like to hear His words and His desire.' Then she stands up, dressed and adorned in immaculate modesty.

Then He says: 'Welcome, my most dear one.' From the tone of the words she recognised that every soul that serves God in grace is most dear to Him. Then He said: 'I must protect you from both my desire

---

153 Cf. p. 76, n. 83.

and yours.' This desire is inexpressible. Then He said: 'Take this crown of the virgins.' Then the crown left Him and settled on her head; it shone as if it were of pure gold. This crown had a double function, for it was also the crown of love. Then Our Lord said: 'This crown shall be displayed in front of all the heavenly host.' Then she asked: 'Lord, will You receive my soul tomorrow when I have received Your holy Body?' 'No,' He said, 'you shall become even richer through suffering.' 'Lord, what should I be doing in this convent?' 'You shall illumine them, and teach them, and shall remain with them in great honour.' Then she thought: 'Ah, now you are alone here with Our Lord.'

While she was thinking this, she saw two angels standing beside her who were marked out by their magnificence, as secular princes are from other people who are poor. Then she said: 'How will I now hide myself?' Then they said: 'We shall bring you from suffering to suffering, from virtue to virtue, from knowledge to knowledge, from love to love.' That a sinful mouth should and must report all this weighs heavily on me and yet, before God and out of obedience, I do not dare not do it. May I keep a sense of mortal shame and godly fear all my days!

VII, 10. This happened at a time of great trouble

I prayed to Our Lord God about the distress of war and the many sins of the world. Then Our Lord answered thus, saying: 'The stench of sin which rises from out of the abyss of Earth right up to Heaven disgusts me; if it were possible, it would drive me out. Sin drove me out once before; then I came in humility and served the world until my death; now that cannot happen again. Now, because of sin, I must from time to time assert my justice.' 'Dear Lord, what should we wretched people now do?' Then Our Lord said: 'You should humble yourselves under the alarming hand of almighty God and fear Him in all that you do. I shall still save my people, that is my friends, from all distress. Communal prayer satisfies my heart. I shall reveal how I am disposed. I like to hear the prayer of religious people who pray from the heart: *Adiutorium nostrum in nomine domini. Laudate dominum omnes gentes. Gloriatur et filius. Regnum mundi. Eructavit cor. Quem vidi. Gloria patri et filio.*'[154] 'Lord heavenly Father, accept

---

154 'Our help is in the name of the Lord. Praise the Lord, all you nations. And the Son is glorified. The kingdom of the world. My heart leapt up. Whom I saw. Glory be to the Father and the Son.' These are all reponses in the Divine Office sung on various feast days. Cf. Neumann (1993: 147f.)

Your service and Your praise from Your sad children and free Your people from this present distress and free us from all our bonds except for the bonds of love. May they never be taken from us!'

VII, 14. Of God's choosing and blessing

Another night, when I was at my prayer and full of longing and was expecting nothing, then I became aware of Our Lord. He was standing in the cemetery and had arrayed before Him the entire community in the order they had entered the convent. Then Our Lord said to them: 'I have chosen you, if you choose me, then I will give you something.' Then I said: 'Lord, what will you give them?' Then He said: 'I shall make shining mirrors out of them on Earth, so that all who see them shall know their life in them;[155] and in Heaven I shall make them bright mirrors, so that everyone who sees them shall know that I have chosen them.' Then Our Lord raised His hand and blessed them saying: 'I bless you with myself, choose me in all your thoughts.' Those who have chosen Our Lord in all their thoughts are the blessed, who praise Our Lord as is fitting. Then I said: 'They will ask me, how you manifested Yourself to me.' Then He said: 'There are some among them who know me.'

VII, 21. How a person should examine their heart before they go to God's table

You want teaching from me and yet I myself am uneducated. That which you constantly thirst for you can find a thousand times in your books.

When I, miserable wretch, go forward and am to receive the Body of Our Lord, then I look at the face of my soul in the mirror[156] of my sins. In it I see myself, how I have lived, how I am living now and how I am going to live. In this mirror of my sins I see nothing but woe and more woe. Then I cast my eyes to the ground and weep and lament as much as I can that eternal, incomprehensible God is so good that He is willing to lower Himself into the filthy mire[157] of my heart. And thus I think that it would only be right and proper if my body were to be dragged to the gallows like a thief who had stolen from his rightful master the precious treasure of purity, which God gave me in holy baptism. We shall lament all the days of our life that

155 Cf. p. 29, n. 6.
156 Cf. p. 29, n. 6.
157 Cf. p. 40, n. 23.

we have often blackened ourselves; Lord, may You, as a father, forgive us that. If a person has a sin that they have neither confessed nor want to confess, then they should not receive God's Body.

Now I shall approach true hope, and thank God that I was ever noticed and that a wretched person like myself may receive the body of God. Now I shall go to God's table with joy and I shall receive that same bloodied Lamb that wanted to hang on the holy cross with His five holy wounds, bloody and untended. How fortunate we are that this ever happened! In His holy passion I shall forget all my sorrow. Then we go with joy and hearts full of love and with an open soul, and receive our Love, the dearest Love of our hearts, and lay Him in our soul as in a lovely crib, and sing His praise and honour for that first hardship that He willingly suffered when He lay in the manger. Then we bow to Him with our soul and with our five senses and thank our Love and say: 'Lord, I thank You for Yourself. Now I beg of You, dear Love, that You might give me Your jewels so that I may have a pure life, free of all sin. Lord, where shall I then lay You down? What I have I will give You. I want to lay You down on my cot. The cot is all suffering. When I think of Your suffering then I forget mine. You should bed down my cheek, Lord. The pillow for my cheek is the sorrow of my heart that I am not ready at all times to accept Your gifts of suffering. This, Lord, is my whole lament. The cover of this bed[158] is my desire, in which I am wrapped. If You wish to calm me, Lord, then do my will and give me the sinners, who are in a state of mortal sin; then You will delight my soul. Lord, what shall we say about love while we are lying so close to one another in the bed of my suffering? I have received You, Lord, as You arose from the dead. Dear Love of my heart, now comfort me, that, pure, I might stand by You always. Great happiness shall follow. Give me, Lord, the guilty souls from Purgatory, even if the ransom money is too much for me. Now I have received You, Lord, as You ascended into Heaven. Now, most Beloved, You should not spare me too much. I must some day die of love;[159] You cannot soothe me any other way, Lord. Give me, Lord, and take from me, Lord, all that You wish, grant me just this one wish, that I might die of love in love. Amen.'

---

158 Cf. p. 30, n. 7.
159 This sounds like an echo of the line from Mechthild's early song 'I would gladly die of love' (II, 2 [p. 37]), the line that she sees embroidered on her cloak in her vision of John the Baptist celebrating Mass (II, 4 [p. 40]).

VII, 28. Of the distress of a war

I was ordered with a holy earnestness to pray for the distress that there is now in the lands of Saxony and Thuringia.[160] When I busied myself with this in prayers of praise and petition, Our dear Lord did not wish to receive me and maintained a grave silence. I had to endure this for seventeen days in loving patience. Then I said to Our dear Lord: 'Ah, dear Lord, when will that welcome hour come when You are prepared to allow me to pray for this distress?' Then Our Lord revealed Himself to me and said: 'The delightful dawn, aflame with colour, that is, the poor people who are suffering so much distress at the moment. After this the everlasting sun of everlasting light shall rise on them, shining upon them with everlasting joy after this distress. As the sparkling sun climbs towards midday and reaches its zenith, they shall be sanctified and transfigured.

There are some in the army who are there through coercion and fear; I shall let them be captured and their lives taken so that they might come to me. Those who caused this war are more dreadful in themselves and more horrendous in their deeds than if they were to dare to lay hold of the images in my church.' Then I understood that eternal death follows for those foot soldiers that loot and pillage in the streets; if there were no war they would be thieves and swindlers. But, as is always the way, the bad people make the blessed good. Hence God must love His own through suffering, otherwise He cannot win them to Him. Thus God told me about the benefit of this war and I do not know when or where it shall come to an end.

I know for sure that I am to continue to gladden the hearts of God's friends. I know for sure that God will never forget what God's friends are suffering, for He is their succour and their comfort in all their distress. Therefore we should fight and suffer willingly and gladly. Then we shall sparkle and shine before God.

VII, 35. Of the seven psalms

Dear Lord Jesus Christ, I recite these holy seven psalms in praise and in honour of all Your holy suffering, in which You were ready to die for my sake on the holy cross. Dear Love, I beg You that, when the time comes for me to die in accordance with Your will, You will

---

[160] Schmidt (1995: 397, n. 292) identifies this fighting as the military campaigns of King Gustav Adolf of Nassau which took place in 1294. Neumann (1954/64: 197ff.), however, points to the fighting between the Landgrave Albrecht of Thuringia and his sons Friedrich and Dietrich in 1281. Both arguments are plausible, though Neumann's has won greater currency.

come to me then as a faithful doctor to his child; and give me then a holy sickness in which I may prepare myself with the right thoughts and with true Christian faith. *Domine ne in furore.*[161]

I beg you, most beloved Lord, that You might then come as my most dear friend in my hour of need and bring me then, Lord, to such true remorse that all my sins will be wiped out so that after this life I shall be light hearted. *Beati quorum remissa.*[162]

I beg you, most beloved Lord, that You might then come as a faithful confessor to his dear friend and bring me the true light, the gift of your Holy Spirit, in which I might examine and know myself, and lament all my sins from the bottom of my heart in the very holy hope that my tongue might not be tied by all my sins and that I shall be found pure; and give me then, Lord, Your own Body that I might then, dear Love, receive it with as much love as a human heart is capable of, so that You might be food for the journey of my solitary soul along the way and so that I, most Beloved, might remain Your dear companion in eternal life. Amen. *Domine ne in furore.*[163]

I beg you, dear Lord, that You might come as a loyal brother to his dear sister and bring me the holy armour, with which my soul will be made ready, so that my enemies cannot injure me when they wish to complain about me, and so that they may be ashamed of all they have done against me. *Miserere mei deus.*[164]

I beg you, Lord, that You might come to me as a faithful father to his dear child and watch over my end; when I can no longer speak with my sinful mouth then speak to my soul inwardly that you might comfort her and protect her for ever and so that I shall be gladdened and not saddened; I beg this of You, Lord, through Your generous kindness. Amen. *Domine, exaudi orationem et clamor.*[165]

I beg you, Lord, that You might send Your Virgin Mother, whom I cannot do without, that she might fulfil what I have long wished for

---

161   'O Lord, rebuke me not in thine anger' (Psalm 6: 1). I quote from the Vulgate version and consequently my numbering of the Psalms is in accordance with the Vulgate ordering. Most Catholic Bibles follow the Vulgate scheme, whereas most non-Catholic Bibles follow the Hebrew Masoretic text. The numbering in the Vulgate and in the Hebrew Masoretic texts is identical as far as Psalm 9, but thereafter the enumeration of the latter is generally higher by one number than it is in the former. The translations into English are from the King James' Bible.

162   'Blessed is he whose transgression is forgiven' (Psalm 31: 1).

163   'O Lord, rebuke me not in thy wrath' (Psalm 38: 1).

164   'Have mercy upon me, O God' (Psalm 50: 1).

165   'Hear my prayer, O Lord, and let my cry come unto thee' (Psalm 101: 1).

and protect my poor soul from all her enemies. *De profundis clamo.*[166]

I beg You, Jesus, dear Young Man, Child of the pure Virgin, that You might then come as my dearest Bridegroom and enrich me then as noble bridegrooms do when they give their brides a grand morning gift[167] and welcome me then on the arm of Your love and cover me with the cloak of Your abiding desire. How fortunate I shall be for evermore, for then I shall be liberated! If we were to think often of the hour when He will reveal His noble countenance to us, then all our arrogance would fall away. Then my soul shall have all her delight. That for which I yearn can never be mine on earth in the way that I wish it. *Domine, exaudi orationem meam auribus percipe.*[168]

VII, 36. Of a spiritual convent[169]

I implored God to let me know, if it were His will, whether I could stop writing. Why? Because I know that I am as insignificant and unworthy as I was more than thirty years ago, when I first had to start writing. Then Our Lord showed me a little bag in His hand and said: 'I still have some herbs.' Then I said: 'Lord, I don't recognise these herbs.' Then He said: 'You certainly will when you see them; with them one can minister to the sick, invigorate the healthy, wake the dead, sanctify the good.'

After this I saw a spiritual convent that was built of virtues.

The abbess is true love and has a very holy mind, with which she watches eagerly over the community in body and soul; this is all to the honour of God. She gives them much holy instruction, which is always God's will; through this her own soul becomes free.

The chaplain of love is divine humility, which is always subordinate to love; thus pride must fall by the wayside.

The prioress is the holy peace of God; her good will is granted patience so that she might teach the community with divine wisdom. Whatever she turns her attention to is always to God's honour.

The sub-prioress is kindness; it is her business to gather together all the little failings and eliminate them with goodness. Whatever the transgression, we should not harbour it in our spirit for long; thus God increases the goodness of mankind. The chapter should incor-

---

[166] 'Out of the depths have I cried unto thee' (Psalm 129: 1).
[167] That is, a gift given to a bride by her husband after the wedding night.
[168] 'Hear my prayer, O Lord, give ear to my supplications' (Psalm 142: 1).
[169] Allegories of this sort were common in contemporary literature. Cf. Schmidt (1995: 400, n. 298 and Ruh (1993: 259 and n. 33).

porate four things, that is the revelation of holiness inherent in the worship of God.[170] Its gentle work does much to harm enemies and to honour God; it may rejoice in this greatly. It should guard against vainglory and should assist others to honour. If they serve eagerly, then God shall reward them accordingly.

The choirmistress is hope; she fills us with holy, humble devotion so that the singing of the helpless heart before God sounds so beautiful that God loves the notes that sing in the heart. Whoever sings with her in this way shall succeed with her in heavenly love.

The schoolmistress is wisdom, who diligently teaches the ignorant with good will; for this she is honoured before good people. The convent is sanctified and honoured by the diligent and willing teaching of the helpless poor.

The mistress of the cellar pours out helpful gifts in abundance; by performing her office with divine joy, she acquires a holy temperament as a divine gift. All those who wish something from her should be restrained and moderate and ever uncomplaining. Then the sweet gift of God shall flow into their hearts. Those who assist her shall always, like her, receive the sweet gifts of God.

The mistress of the chamber is generosity, who always likes to do good in proper measure. She gives what she has with a kindly will. For this God bestows special grace on her. Those to whom she gives thank God with holy fervour; there is room for Him in her heart like noble wine in an untainted keg.

The mistress of the sick is flowing mercy, that always strives to be indefatigably ready to serve the sick, with help and cleanliness, with refreshment and cheerfulness, with comfort and kindness. God rewards her so that she always serves gladly. Whoever assists her shall receive the same from God.

The mistress of the gate is vigilance, who is always filled with a holy desire to do whatever is asked of her; her work is not in vain, for she easily comes to God. When she wants to pray, then God is with her in holy stillness to ease the sorrow of her heart. On those occasions when the going is tough, holy obedience, to whom she is joyfully subject, smoothes her path in all things.

The mistress of discipline is the observance of holy custom. She shall always burn in heavenly freedom like a candle that is never extinguished. In this way we shall bear all the sorrow of our heart until we reach a holy end.

---

170   The text is obscure at this point. Cf. Neumann (1993: 155).

The provost is divine obedience and not sinful obedience. All virtues are subordinate to him.

In this way the convent may exist in God.

Whoever would enter this convent shall always live here and in the eternal life with divine joy. Blessed are they who stay therein!

VII, 39. How the devils fight and hound one another, and gnash their teeth whenever a loving soul, burning with the love of God, departs this world

The good person who, to the best of their ability, follows God with all virtues, is fortunate indeed that they were ever born; their soul is set free in love. At the end of their life the holy angels shall come and receive the pure Soul with indescribable love into heavenly bliss and lead her away from here with joy and bring her to God with great praise.

The fiends that arrived there from Hell are frustrated in all their efforts; they had come there filled with hatred and fury. When they see that they are not to have their way, how they fight and hound one another, how they gnash their teeth, how then they howl and whine, because they fear the dreadful pain that their masters shall inflict on them for having lost the Soul. This is how they blame one another: 'You wretch, it was your fault.' 'Shut up, comrade, I never found any great impatience in her. Whenever I shot evil thoughts at her, remorse was at once her companion.' 'That whispering with the confessors robs us all of our honour. There were many others like us into whose care she was specially entrusted. How can we show ourselves at court now?' 'Alas, master, what were you thinking of that you entrusted this person to us? We could detect no sin of any moment in her.' 'Whenever I led her into temptation, she would start to weep; my comrades and I were quite unable to trip her up. She drove me away with weeping, she singed my hair and claws with sighing; I could never get near her.' 'Her obedience was so great that there was never her like. That is why she has rightly been taken from us. This is as damaging to us as it could be. All her good deeds glowed from within with divine love, because all her good deeds were performed with good intentions.' Their master speaks thus: 'You come to court disgraced, masters. I entrusted her to you: the pain I shall inflict on you for this will never be lifted from you. You shall not associate with those people with whom I should so like to be with, if I were allowed the honour. Now you must lie in Hell here with me; that shall be your penance. I shall send out great masters to darken the understanding of good people. If only we could destroy the great zeal that they have for God, then all honour would be ours, the young would follow them and so the likes of us would be increased. If only one of those souls could be mine, which burn so brightly with the love of God, I would crown myself with her and would reward myself for my persistent efforts and thus would all the sorrow of my heart be assuaged.' 'Say goodbye to your arrogant desire, you long for what you have never had and never shall have, whatever ill may attend you. All the blessed Christians who in their hearts ache for God are so steeped in and suffused with love that they radiate holy virtues and in all their deeds are on fire with love. You know very well that it does you no good at all to tempt them so severely. They simply wait until that moment when they can praise God. However much you stalk them with cunning, they are ready with praise.' It is beyond description how he, in his bonds, then growled and raged and gnashed his teeth.

Lord God, we thank You, give us a holy end. One of the greatest joys that the Soul has is that she sees and knows that the fiends fight one another and do penance in Hell which gives them much pain; and so the Soul has escaped them with joy and shall wear the eternal crown because of the suffering they inflicted on her.

VII, 41. How a brother of the Order of Preachers was seen

There was a religious man I knew forty years ago; at that time religious people were true and fired with love. Inwardly, he grew in spirituality and in piety and, outwardly, did much holy work for Our Lord. He has now passed on from here. Then I prayed to Our Lord as a Christian for his soul,[171] that God might forgive him any sin he might be guilty of. Then I saw first of all a brightness that God had prepared for him; I did not find him in it. Then my soul grew sad.

After that, on another occasion when I was praying for him, I found him in a fiery cloud. Then he begged that he might be forgiven. Then I spoke to Our dear Lord with all my might: 'Ah dear Lord, grant me that I may reward bad with good.' Then he rose up in the cloud and said: 'O Lord, how great is Your power, how just is Your truth.' Then I said: 'Well now, how are things with you?' Then he said: 'They are as you see.' 'Where does this suffering come from?' The Soul:[172] 'Holy hypocrites made false accusations to me about innocent people. I made these innocents make amends and had

---

171   Cf. V, 5 (p. 92); V, 15 (p. 89).
172   That is, of the brother of the Order of Preachers.

a poor opinion of them; that is where my suffering comes from. Alas, if only I had one more sigh!'[173] I could not oblige him in this, for he had also been a little thoughtless towards me.

On a third occasion I prayed for him. Then he moved on in bliss. Then Our dear Lord came to meet him and said to him: 'It is wicked people who have made your path after your death so long and so difficult. You have followed me reverently and served me faithfully; you shall wear the crown of virgins, the crown of justice and the crown of truth.'

Then, radiant, he rose over eight choirs and touched the ninth; then I no longer saw him. If false liars had not worked on him, then he would have passed on to eternal joy without any suffering. In trusting them he hurt himself.

VII, 51. A prayer against sins of omission

I, the most insignificant, the most wretched, the most unworthy of all mankind, I implore, I beseech you, Lord Heavenly Father, Lord Jesus Christ, Lord Holy Spirit, Lord Holy Trinity, that today You might forgive me for all the sins of omission which I have committed in Your holy service, not just because of self-interest and need, but because of my sinful wickedness, which I could have put an end to, had I wanted. Now receive, Lord, this small improvement that I make for You with my will and for the honour of Your dear Mother and all the saints, who are celebrated today in the holy Christian Church; and in praise and honour of all God's holy in their blessedness, which has brought them to you, dear Lord. Now help me, dear Lord, to such a change in my life, that, through living in holiness, I may become the companion of Your saints on earth, that I might have the company of Your saints in Your kingdom before Your sublime countenance, together with all those who wish me to pray for them.

VII, 57. A little about Paradise

This was revealed and I saw what Paradise was like. I found no end to its breadth and its length.[174] First I came to a place between this world and the beginning of Paradise; there I saw trees, foliage and wonderful grass, but no weeds. Some trees bore apples, but most of them had only foliage with a fine scent. Swift running waters flow

---

173   That is, if only he were still alive and thus able to repent his sin through the regret he feels. Purgatory is a place of expiation and punishment rather than penitence.

174   In the structure of Mechthild's universe, Purgatory is complemented by Paradise, just as Heaven is complemented by Hell.

through there and the wind blows from the south to the north. There in the waters earthly sweetness was blended with heavenly bliss. There the air was sweeter than I can describe. There was neither beast nor bird, for God had given this to mankind alone so that they might live in comfort there.

Then I saw two men in there, these were Enoch and Elijah.[175] Enoch was sitting and Elijah lying on the earth in deep devotion. Then I spoke to Enoch. I asked whether they lived as human beings do. Then he said: 'We eat a little of the apples and drink a little of the water so that our bodies might remain alive, but the greatest thing is the power of God.' I asked him: 'How did you come here?' 'I came here not knowing how I came here and how things were with me before I was sitting here.' I asked him about his prayer. 'We pray out of faith and hope.' I asked him how he was, whether anything bothered him about being there. Then he said: 'All is well with me and nothing is wrong.' 'Are you afraid at all of the battle which is yet to take place in the world?' 'God shall arm me with His power, so that I shall be well able to do battle.' 'Do you pray for Christianity at all?' 'I pray that God may free her of sin and bring her into His kingdom.' Elijah stood up; now his face was handsome, fiery, with a heavenly hue, his hair like white wool. They were dressed as poor men who go in search of their bread with a staff in their hand. Then I asked Elijah how he prayed for Christianity. 'I pray with compassion and humility and with faithfulness and obedience.' 'Do you pray at all for the souls?'[176] 'Yes, when I intercede for them, their suffering is lessened; when I request it, their suffering also vanishes.' 'Will they be redeemed at all?' 'Yes, many of them.' 'Why has God brought you here?' 'So that we might assist Christianity and God before the Day of Judgement.'

I saw Paradise in two parts. I have spoken about the earthly part. The heavenly part is up above, protecting the earthly part from all storms. In the uppermost part are those souls who were not deserving of Purgatory, but who have not yet entered God's kingdom. They shimmer in bliss as air does in sunlight. Until they enter the kingdom of God they shall have neither power nor honour, neither reward nor crown.

When all of Earth shall come to an end and earthly Paradise no longer exists, then heavenly Paradise too shall come to an end after

---

175 Cf. IV, 27; VI, 15.
176 That is, the souls in Purgatory.

God has held His judgement; all those who wish to come to God shall live together in the one house. There will no longer be an infirmary; whoever enters God's kingdom shall be free of all sickness. Praise be to Jesus Christ who has given us His kingdom.

VII, 58. Of Saint Gabriel[177]

Holy Angel Gabriel, think of me. I entrust you with the message of my desire. Tell my dear Lord Jesus Christ how lovesick I am for Him. If I am ever to recover, then it is He who must be my physician. You can tell Him in truth that I can no longer bear it that the wounds He has dealt me Himself are left untreated and unbound. He has wounded me unto death. If He leaves me now without treatment then I shall never recover. Even if all the mountains were balm for wounds and all the waters a medicinal drink and all blossoming trees a healing bandage, I should never recover; He must lay Himself in the wounds of my soul.

Holy Angel Gabriel, think of me. I entrust this message of love to you. May this letter of love awaken the senses of whosoever would love and follow God.

VII, 59. How the message reached God

I have clearly perceived the truth in my spirit, my message has reached God. The reply which should come to me is so great, so powerful, so unfathomable, so manifold, so blissful and so brilliant that I am unable to receive it for as long as I am of this Earth, that is unless I escape this mortal coil for just a little while, so that I am not permanently lodged in it. Now I must stop talking about this mighty reply; I could not receive any more that could be spoken of openly. In as far as a poor creature like myself was able, I saw St Gabriel in the heavenly heights standing before God in blissful honour. He was dressed in new robes of fiery love given to him as a reward for delivering a true message so honourably; I saw his face fiery with love and radiantly bright. He was surrounded and suffused by the Godhead. I could neither hear nor understand his words, for I still have the likeness of an earthly fool.

---

177 Tobin (1998: 367, n. 61) compares this chapter to a conventional form of courtly-love lyric, the *Botenlied* ['messenger's song'], in which the speaker addresses a messenger concerning the object of his or her love and asks him to bear the message of love to the loved one.

VII, 60. How the Child was seen

In the night, on which the Son of God was born, the Child was seen wrapped in poor pieces of cloth, bound by swaddling bands. The Child lay alone on the rough straw before two animals. Then I spoke to the Mother: 'Ah, dear Lady, how long must this dear Child lie alone like this? When will you take Him onto your lap?' Then Our Lady said that she never let the Child out of her sight. She reached out her hands to Him and said: 'He shall lie on this straw for the seven hours of the day and night. His heavenly Father wishes it so.' It was clear to me then that the heavenly Father was well pleased with this. I spoke to the Child on behalf of those who had entrusted themselves to me. Then a voice came from the Child, although He never moved His mouth: 'If they will hold me in their thoughts, then I shall hold them in my grace. I have nothing to give them other than my body and life eternal.'

In presepio[178] the Child lay on rough straw; its heavenly Father wished it so.

VII, 64. How God serves mankind

This is how a beggar woman speaks in her prayer to God: 'Lord, I thank You that in Your love You have taken from me all earthly riches and that You now clothe and feed me with the wealth of others, for everything in my possession that clings and gives pleasure to my heart must become foreign to me. Lord, I thank You that, since You have taken my eyesight from me, You now serve me with the eyes of others. Lord, I thank You that, since You have taken the strength from my hands, You now serve me with the hands of others. Lord, I thank You that, since You have taken the strength of my heart, You now serve me with the hearts of others.

Lord, I pray to You for them, that You might reward them on Earth with Your divine love so that they might beseech You and serve You with all virtue until they come to a holy end.

All those who abandon everything with a pure heart for the sake of God's love are arch-beggars; on the Last Day they shall sit in judgement with Jesus, our Redeemer. Lord, may You transform in me and in all sinners all that I bring to You in lament. Lord, may You grant to me and all imperfect religious people everything that I ask for the sake of Your own honour. Lord, whatever else I might do, leave

---

[178] 'In a stable'.

undone and suffer, may Your praise never be silent in my heart.'
Amen.

VII, 65. How God adorns the Soul with suffering

At all times, when virgins are dressed as pleases their Bridegroom,
then they need nothing other than their wedding clothes; that is, they
are racked with pain in sickness, days of suffering, temptation and in
much heartfelt sorrow; we find much of this in sinful Christianity.
These are the wedding clothes of the loving Soul. But the workday
clothes are fasting, keeping vigil, doing acts of penance, confessing,
sighing, weeping, praying, fearing sin, harshly disciplining the
senses and the body in God for God, sweet hope and a constantly
loving desire and a heart that is constantly prayerful in all its doings.
These are the workday clothes of a good person. When we are sick
we wear our wedding clothes, but when we are well, then we wear
our workday clothes.

This is how the tormented Body speaks to the estranged Soul:
'When will you fly on the wings of your desire into the blissful
heights to Jesus, your eternal Love? Thank Him, Lady, on my behalf
that, although I am wretched and unworthy, He wanted to be mine
when He came into this exile and assumed our humanity; and entreat
Him to keep me guiltless in His grace until we reach a holy end,
when you, most dear Soul, will turn away from me.'

The Soul: 'Ah, my most dear prison in which I have been
shackled, I thank you for everything in which you have followed me;
although you have often caused me to be sad, nonetheless you have
often come to my aid; you shall be relieved of all your distress on the
Day of Judgement. If you will now stand firm and hold fast to sweet
hope, then we shall lament no longer, then we shall be content with
everything that God has done with us.'

Obedience is a holy bond; it binds the Soul to God and the Body to
Jesus and the five Senses to the Holy Spirit. The longer it binds, the
more the Soul loves; the less the Body thinks of itself the more beautifully its works shine before God and before people of good will.

Interpretive Essay

'With the Eyes of my Soul': Bearing Witness

Introduction

Throughout *The Flowing Light of the Godhead* Mechthild exhibits an acute and many-facetted awareness of herself as both the author and the subject of her text in her efforts to bear witness to her visionary and mystical experiences within the limitations set by her gender, education, social position and historical location:

> Ah Lord, if I were an educated, religious man and You had worked this singular great wonder in him, then You would have had eternal honour from that. Now, how can anyone believe of You that You have built a golden house in a filthy quagmire and really live there with Your mother and with all creatures and with Your entire heavenly host? Lord, the wisdom of this world cannot find You in this. (II, 26 [p. 48])

One of the principal features of the author's self-projection in the *FL* is the emphasis she places on her sense of humility:

> Then I, poor wretch, went to my father confessor, trembling in humble shame and told him all this and begged also for his guidance. Then he said that I should proceed joyfully; God, who had drawn me to Him, would look after me well. Then he instructed me to do what often gives me cause to weep for shame, for I am acutely aware of my own unworthiness; that is, he ordered a pitiful woman to write this book out of the heart and mouth of God. Thus, this book has come lovingly from God and is not drawn from human senses.
>
> (IV, 2 [p. 73])

However, despite the self-effacement of this modesty topos, Mechthild is pervasively present in and central to her text. In conceptual terms the *FL* deals with the intersection of Mechthild's personal story with the master story of Christian salvation history.[1] In this metaphysical narrative the temporal and the eternal, the physical and the spiritual are contiguous; Mechthild conducts a dialogue with

---

[1] Cf. Wright (1988: 83).

God, herself, her contemporaries and her readers. She is the location where the temporal and the eternal meet.

The Soul, the Body and the Senses

In the execution of this dialogue, Mechthild's identity as narrator oscillates between fragmentation and integration. She may speak as a first- or third-person narrator, or through aspects of herself as the Soul, the Body and the Senses. The ancient rhetorical device of personification enables Mechthild to reveal to her readers in a vivid manner the dynamics of her spiritual life. The personifications of the Body, Senses and Soul have as much presence in the narrative as do Mechthild's other interlocutors, be they celestial, infernal, biblical, historical or contemporary.[2] The Soul, as the key protagonist in Mechthild's metaphysical narrative, is introduced in the very first chapter (I, 1) in dialogue with Love. The Body makes its entrance in the following chapter, in conflict with the Soul as the consequence of the Soul's absence from the Body in her experience of mystical union:

> Then the Body says: 'Well, Lady, now where have you been? You come back so full of love, beautiful and strong, free and sharp-witted. Your going robbed me of my sense of taste and smell, of my colour and all my strength.' Then she says: 'Shut up, murderer, stop your moaning! I'll always be on my guard against you . . .' (I, 2 [p. 28])

The suffering inflicted on the Body when the Soul enjoys mystical union is reiterated once more in I, 5:

> My body is in prolonged torment, my soul is in elated bliss, for she has both seen and embraced her Lover fully. [. . .] Then the Body says to the Soul: 'Where have you been? I can't take any more.' Then the Soul says: 'Shut up, you're a fool. I want to be with my love even if that were to mean the end of you. I am His delight, He is my torment.' (I, 5 [p. 29])

In the account Mechthild gives in Book IV of her first mystical experience at the age of twelve and the consequences this had for her subsequent spiritual development,[3] she describes her body as the enemy of her soul and lists the measures she has to take to subdue the body:

---

2 Cf. Andersen (2000: 195ff.). Mechthild also engages with personifications of abstract concepts, e.g. 'Constancy', 'Desire', Knowledge', 'Love', 'Pain'.
3 Cf. the Introduction (p. 3).

When I took up the religious life and took leave of the world, then I looked at my body; it was well armed against my poor soul with mighty strength in abundance and with all the power of nature. [. . .] Then I had to be constantly in great fear and throughout my youth had to strike my body with heavy defensive blows: these were sighing, weeping, confessing, fasting, keeping vigil, flagellation and constant worship. These were the weapons of my soul with which I overcame my body so greatly that in twenty years there was never a time that I was not tired, sick and weak, first of all from repentance and suffering, after that from holy desire and from spiritual effort and, in addition, from many heavy days of physical sickness. (IV, 2 [pp. 72f.])

The faculties of the Body, however, are presented as less of a threat to the Soul. In the exemplary account of the Soul's progress to union with the Godhead (I, 44), the Senses are conceived as the chamberlains of the Soul, who seek to offer advice and to warn the Soul of the risks they perceive in the union of the soul with the Godhead:

'O Lady, if you go there, then we shall be completely blinded, for the Godhead, as you well know, is so fiery hot that all the fire and incandescence, in which Heaven and all the saints burn and glow, streams from His divine breath and out of His human mouth on the advice of the Holy Spirit. How could you last even an hour there?' (I, 44 [p. 35])

In contrast to her attitude to the Body in I, 2 and I, 5, the Soul here adopts a conciliatory and constructive tone: ' "Now don't be too distressed! You shall still advise me; when I return I shall be in need of your guidance, for this Earth is full of snares." ' (I, 44 [p. 36]). Although the dichotomy of the Soul and the Body persists throughout the *FL*, the reader is nonetheless reminded on occasion of the integrated identity of the Soul, Body and Senses in the persona of the narrator. This is expressed forcibly in the unified focus of IV, 13 where Mechthild makes a succinct, categorical statement in a chapter of just a few lines about what determines and motivates her to write:

I cannot, nor will not, write, unless I see with the eyes of my soul and hear with the ears of my eternal spirit and feel the power of the Holy Spirit in all the members of my body.

(IV, 13 [p. 77])

This sense of holistic unity recurs in the final chapter of the *FL*. Just as the *FL* opens with the Soul and the Body in dialogue, so too it

closes. However, the conflict of I, 2 and I, 5 is resolved in VII, 65 in a harmonious reconciliation. The Soul says to the 'tormented' Body:
'Ah, my most dear prison in which I have been shackled, I thank you for everything in which you have followed me; although you have often caused me to be sad, nonetheless you have often come to my aid; you shall be relieved of all your distress on the Last Day. If you will now stand firm and hold fast to sweet hope, then we shall lament no longer, then we shall be content with everything that God has done with us.' (VII, 65 [p. 139])
The nature of the integral identity of the Body, Soul and Senses is expressed through the drawing of a correspondence between them and the three aspects of the indivisible Trinity:
Obedience is a holy bond; it binds the Soul to God and the Body to Jesus and the five Senses to the Holy Spirit. The longer it binds, the more the Soul loves; the less the Body thinks of itself the more beautifully its works shine before God and before people of good will. (VII, 65 [p. 139])
Trinitarian analogies abound in Mechthild's writings. On a number of occasions her whole person is described in Trinitarian terms, creating, as it were, a symmetry in the narrative between herself and the Godhead. Thus, for example, in her exemplary description of the path of the loving Soul to mystical union she says: 'I must leave all things to go to God, who is my Father by nature, my Brother in His humanity, my Bridegroom in love and I His Bride eternally' (I, 44 [p. 36]) and in her old age God says to Mechthild: "Your childhood was a companion to my Holy Spirit; your youth was a bride to my Humanity; your old age is now a wife to my Godhead" (VII, 3 [p. 124]). Underlying the symmetry of the triadic correspondence between aspects of Mechthild and the Trinity is a complete identification of her whole being with the Trinity: ' "Lord, heavenly Father, you are my heart; Lord Jesus Christ, you are my body; Lord Holy Spirit, you are my breath . . ." ' (V, 6, 9–10).[4]

---

4   McGinn (1998: 233f.) comments that not only did Mechthild, like a number of the other women mystics of the thirteenth century, emphasise 'the exemplary or preexistent reality of the soul in the Trinity', but she also had in her understanding of the heavenly reward of the body 'a profoundly optimistic view of corporeal existence, despite the presence of some of the negative language about the body to be expected in any medieval author.' Cf. Hollywood (1995: 73ff.) for an analysis of the theological thought underlying Mechthild's representation of the Body and the Soul and the right ordering of human existence through will.

Fragmentation and integration

A fluctuation between the fragmentation and integration of the narrator's persona within the compass of a single chapter is a distinctive feature of Mechthild's narrative strategy.[5] The following analysis of I, 2, the first account in the *FL* of a state of ecstasy, may serve to illustrate some of the potential of this constant shifting of narrative perspective. This chapter opens in the third person with an authoritative statement:

> The true greeting of God, which issues forth from the heavenly flood out of the fountain of the flowing Trinity, has such mighty force that it deprives the Body of all its strength and reveals the Soul to herself so that she sees herself in the likeness of the saints and is then bathed in radiance.
>
> (I, 2 [p. 27])

The narrator goes on to describe how the Soul leaves the Body and her intimate and loving reception by God. Dramatically, a first-person narrator, the author, whom we are tempted to equate with Mechthild, breaks in to address her reader, exclaiming at the enormity of what she is describing: 'Thus they soar further to a wondrous place, of which I neither can nor will speak. It is too difficult, I dare not, for I am a very sinful person. To carry on: . . .' (I, 2 [p. 28]). The third-person narrator continues and reports a loving exchange between the Soul and God in direct speech. Once the experience of mystical union is over, the Soul returns to the Body. There is a sharp exchange between them, reported in direct speech, as the Body complains of the impact of the Soul's absence. The chapter then reverts once more to a third-person narrative with a further authoritative statement, drawn from the incident described:

> This is a greeting that has many channels; it constantly presses out of the flowing God into the poor, parched soul with new insight and new revelation and with particular enjoyment of the new presence. (I, 2, [p. 28])

It concludes with another intervention by the first person narrator who claims the experience for her own, expressing her desire for more of the same. Finally, this first person narrator distinguishes between those who are open to the kind of religious experience described and those who are blind to it:

---

[5]   On Mechthild's use of narrative perspective, see Andersen (2000: 171ff.), Grubmüller (1992), Hollywood (1995: 62ff.), and Kasten (1995).

No one can or may receive this greeting unless they have been outside of themselves and have become nothing. I want to die alive in this greeting; the blindly devout, that is those who love but have no insight, will never be able to ruin this for me. (I, 2, [p. 28f.])

Within the context of such passages as I, 2 that have the *unio mystica* ['mystical union'] as their main focus, the narrator moves at will from describing the loving Soul generically in her relationship with God to actually identifying herself as the loving Soul. Thus, on the one hand the significance of the episode is distilled or abstracted for the reader, but on the other the individuality and immediacy of the experience is maintained in the claiming of it. In her writings Mechthild bears witness to her individual experience, but always with reference, both explicitly and implicitly, to a community of loving souls. In I, 44, for example, she records the path to the experience of *unio mystica* as a way accessible to all loving souls, while also foregrounding her own experience:

'Ah, loving Soul, do you want to know what your path might be like?' 'Yes, dear Holy Spirit, tell me about it.' 'When you have gone beyond the distress of repentance and beyond the pain of confession and beyond the labour of penance and beyond the love of the world [. . .] Dear friend of God, I have written down this path of love for you, may God favour your heart with it! Amen. (I, 44 [pp. 33ff.])

The eyes of the soul
The two principal channels of experiential knowledge that Mechthild presents in the *FL* are the vision and the *unio mystica*. The reports of these experiences are generally presented as independent occurrences, but they can also be fused, as, for example, in the report of the vision of Heaven (III, 1 [pp. 51ff.]).[6] This opens with a description of the author's personal experience of mystical union with God, then moves into a visionary eye-witness account of Heaven and concludes with a vision of the collective mystical union that the community of loving souls in Heaven shall enjoy everlastingly with God. Both the visionary and the mystical experience involve the ecstatic independence of the Soul from the Body.

As a personification, the Soul is endowed with sight, hearing, smell, taste and touch, faculties which correspond to the Body's five

6   Cf. Tax (1979: 115ff.)

senses, although the Soul's spiritual senses clearly function on a different plane. In her autobiographical account in Book IV Mechthild conveys her first ecstatic experience through the faculty of her spiritual sight:[7]

> Then, for the first time, my spirit was transported out of my prayers to between Heaven and air; then I saw with the eyes of my soul in heavenly bliss the beautiful humanity of Our Lord Jesus Christ, and I recognised in His noble countenance the Holy Trinity, the eternity of the Father, the passion of the Son, the sweetness of the Holy Spirit. (IV, 2 [p. 70f.])

On only one earlier occasion in the *FL* does Mechthild refer explicitly to the apprehension of what has been revealed to her through the eyes of her soul.[8] She opens II, 3 with the following:

> The great tongue of the Godhead has spoken many powerful words to me; I have received these with the pitiful ears of my worthlessness; and the greatest light of all has revealed itself to the eyes of my soul, in which I have seen the inexpressible ordering . . . (II, 3, 4–7)

However, all her descriptions of visionary and mystical experiences are implicitly predicated on the witness of her spiritual senses, in particular her sight, as for example:

> I have seen
> With my bright eyes
> Him whom I love
> Standing in my soul (II, 2 [p. 37])

and:

> I have seen a mountain [. . .] the eyes that would see me in this way . . . (II, 21 [p. 43f.])

Following the autobiographical chapter in Book IV, there is a significant increase in explicit references to the 'eyes of the soul'.[9] In contrast to many other visionary writers, Mechthild spends almost no time in the accounts of her visions describing the physical process of moving into an ecstatic state.[10] Instead, on a number of occasions,

---

[7] Schmidt (1985: 131ff.) examines Mechthild's use and interpretation of the spiritual senses with particular reference to the sense of taste.

[8] She does, however, make reference on three occasions to the 'eyes of knowledge' (III, 7, 12–13; III, 12, 13; IV, 18, 56) and on one occasion to 'spiritual ears' (I, 6, 2).

[9] Explicit references to the 'eyes of the soul' in the *FL* occur as follows: II, 3, 6; IV, 2 [p. 70]; IV, 13 [p. 77]; IV, 23, 2–3; V, 35, 59; VI, 1 [p. 105]; VI, 29, 3–4; VI, 31 [p. 115]; VI, 36 [p. 116]; VII, [p. 120]; VII, 7, 28; VII, 37, 34; VII, 48, 71.

[10] Cf. Bochsler (1997: 13ff.).

she uses the phrase 'the eyes of the soul' as a kind of shorthand to alert the reader to the visionary nature of what she is about to report. By extension, Mechthild on occasion explicitly refers to the 'eyes of the body' as a means of highlighting the physical mode of perception in contrast to the spiritual. Thus, for example, in talking about the Annunciation she says of Mary:[11]

> The Virgin was bathed in the light and the angel wore clothing the like of which I have never seen on earth. When she saw the light with the eyes of her body, then she stood up and was afraid. (V, 23 [p. 94])

And later in the same chapter she contrasts Mary's spiritual knowledge with Mary Magdalene's limited understanding:

> Mary, Our Lady, spoke in her thoughts to Our Lord as often as she needed and sometimes His Godhead would answer her and enable her to bear the sorrow of her heart with composure; Mary Magdalene was not at all prepared in this way – when she did not see Our Lord with the eyes of her body, she was inconsolable and during that time her heart was burdened with great distress and pain. She burned in simple love without any higher knowledge of heavenly things until the hour when the Apostles received the Holy Spirit; then for the first time her soul was wounded by the Godhead. (V, 23 [p. 99])

The incidence of reference to the 'eyes of the soul' is particularly high in Books VI and VII. This seems to reflect, as will emerge below, a greater need in Mechthild to insist on the authority of her spiritual senses.

The striking phenomenon of shifting narrative perspective within the context of one chapter, although a characteristic feature of Mechthild's narrative style, particularly in those passages that have as their focus the *unio mystica*, is by no means ubiquitous in the *FL*. There are chapters that are consistently in the first person, where the reader has a sense of an integrated narrator. This is perhaps nowhere greater than in the autobiographical chapter (IV, 2), where the author, the first-person narrator and the subject of the narrative coalesce. In other autobiographical passages in the course of her writings, Mechthild reflects upon the authorship of her book and reveals to her readers some of the creative impulse that results in her writings.[12]

---

[11] Cf. III, 20 [p. 63f.].

[12] For a detailed tracing of Mechthild's reflections on the authorship of the *FL*, see Andersen (2000: 104ff.).

One of her preoccupations, understandably, is how she can verify to her contemporaries the authenticity of what she has recorded. In her unequivocal statement about what determines and motivates her to write (IV, 13), Mechthild cites the evidence of her spiritual eyes as being fundamental: 'I cannot, nor will not, write, unless I see with the eyes of my soul'. Although she also cites the witness of her spiritual ears, from this point on in the *FL* it is the phrase 'with the eyes of my soul' that becomes the hallmark for the authenticity of Mechthild's mystical and visionary experience.

The history of the eyes of the soul topos
In invoking the authority of the 'eyes of the soul' and the 'ears of my eternal spirit' Mechthild was drawing on a conventional topos with a long history. The first expression that we have of the concept of five spiritual senses by analogy with the physical senses is found in the writings of Origen (*c.* 185– *c.* 254).[13] The teaching on the spiritual senses is rooted in an interpretation of biblical passages such as Psalm 34:

8   O taste and see that the Lord is good: blessed is the man
     that trusteth in him.
15 The eyes of the Lord are upon the righteous, and his ears
     are open unto their cry.

And from Paul's letter to the Ephesians (I: 17–18) in which he tells of how he prays to God for them:

17 That the God of our Lord Jesus Christ, the Father of
     glory, may give unto you the spirit of wisdom and revela-
     tion in the knowledge of him:
18 The eyes of your understanding being enlightened; that
     ye may know what is the hope of his calling, and what
     the riches of the glory of his inheritance in the saints.

The doctrine of the spiritual senses was transmitted into Latin western culture where it gained common currency in patristic writings. In a famous and influential passage from the *Confessions* Augustine (354–430) describes his love of God in terms of the five spiritual senses:[14]

---

13 Cf. Schmidt (1985: 132). Origen was the most important theologian and biblical
    scholar of the early Greek church.
14 Augustine is the major Christian theologian of the early Western church. In his
    works, Augustine fused the religion of the New Testament with the Platonic tradi-
    tion of Greek philosophy.

But when I love you, what do I love? It is not the physical beauty nor temporal glory nor the brightness of light dear to earthly eyes, nor the sweet melodies of all kinds of songs, nor the gentle odour of flowers and ointments and perfumes, nor manna or honey, nor limbs welcoming the embraces of the flesh; it is not these I love when I love my God. Yet there is a light I love, and a food, and a kind of embrace when I love my God – a light, voice, odour, food, embrace of my inner man, where my soul is floodlit by light which space cannot contain, where there is sound that time cannot seize, where there is a perfume which no breeze disperses, where there is a taste for food no amount of eating can lessen, and where there is a bond of union that no satiety can part. That is what I love when I love my God. (X. vi [8])

He too talks of the 'eye of the soul' in a passage about ascent to God through introspection:

I entered and with my soul's eye, such as it was, saw above that same eye of my soul the immutable light higher than my mind – not the light of everyday, obvious to anyone, nor a larger version of the same kind which would, as it were, have given out a much brighter light and filled everything with its magnitude. It was not that light, but a different thing, utterly different from all our kinds of light. (VII. x [16])

The concept of the spiritual senses and its justification through reference to biblical passages became widely known in the Middle Ages, helping to shape the medieval apprehension of man's spiritual nature.[15] Some evidence of the currency of this concept in the German-speaking world of the thirteenth century is provided in Rudolf of Biberach's *De septem itineribus aeternitatis*, which was translated into German in the fourteenth century as *Die siben strassen zu got* [The seven roads to God]. In his popular treatise, Rudolf, a Franciscan and near contemporary of Mechthild (*c.* 1270 –1326), included an account of the teaching on the spiritual senses. *The Seven Roads to God* constitutes, as it were, a *summa* [compendium] of mystical theology as it had evolved up to Rudolf's day and is thus illuminating with regard to the sources, transmission and dissemination of many of the central images in the *FL*.[16] In her

---

[15] Cf. Lüers (1926/1966: 89; 129–31) and Schmidt (1982; 1984).

[16] Rudolf draws on the writings of Augustine (354–430), Pseudo-Dionysius (*c.* 500) and his commentators, Gregory the Great (*c.* 540–604), William of St Thierry

edition of *Die siben strassen zu got* Margot Schmidt has highlighted parallels in the use of imagery by Rudolf and Mechthild, not least in the employment of the metaphor of the 'eyes of the soul'.[17]

The spiritual authority of the eyes of the soul

A century earlier, Hildegard of Bingen (1098–1179), Mechthild's great visionary predecessor in the German-speaking world, had reported that she did not apprehend her visions with her physical senses, but rather with the 'eyes of the soul'. In a letter Hildegard wrote in 1175, when she was 77, to the monk Guibert of Gembloux she says of her visions: 'But I hear them not with my physical ears, nor with my heart's thoughts, nor do I perceive them by bringing any of my five senses to bear – but only in my soul.'[18] In his history of western Christian mysticism, Bernard McGinn identifies the emergence of a new element in the twelfth century: 'when some religious leaders, like Rupert of Deutz, Hildegard of Bingen and Joachim of Fiore, began to employ direct visionary encounters with God as modes of authentification for their theological writings'.[19] As is evident from McGinn's comment, both men and women utilised the divine origins of private revelations to legitimise their writings. However, the authority derived from private revelations was to become a particularly pronounced and prevalent feature in the writings of women in the twelfth, thirteenth and fourteenth centuries who were otherwise denied access to positions of sacerdotal authority within the established Church. Mechthild's younger contemporary in the convent at Helfta, Mechthild of Hackeborn (1241– *c.* 1298) reports that God gave her 'His eyes', the light of which so suffused her that she saw, as it were, 'with divine eyes'.[20] In similar vein, the Soul in the *FL* serves as a channel of communication for God: 'You are a light for my eyes, you are a lyre for my ears,

(*c.* 1085–1148), Bernard of Clairvaux (1190–1153), Hugh (d. 1142) and Richard (d. 1173) of St Victor, Thomas Gallus (d. 1246) and Robert Grosseteste (*c.* 1175–1253).

17 Cf. Schmidt (1969: 143ff.). The sole extant manuscript of *Die siben strassen zu got*, Ms 278, is also held in the monastery library at Einsiedeln and is in the same scribal hand as Ms 277, the only complete extant manuscript of the *FL*. Both manuscripts belonged originally to Margaretha zum Goldenen Ring (*c.* 1320– *c.* 1404). She was the daughter of a prosperous merchant, a beguine and a friend of the local Dominicans.

18 The translation is taken from Dronke (1984: 252).

19 McGinn (1998: xiv).

20 Mechthild von Hackeborn, *Liber specialis gratiae* (Bk. II, chap. 34 [p. 179]).

you are a voice for my words (III, 2, 11–12). This definition of the function of Mechthild's soul as an instrument of God is even more forcefully expressed in a further dialogue between God and the Soul just a few chapters later, when God declares: 'I am the light and your breast is the lantern' (III, 12, 15). He explains how the light emanating from Him shall, through the lantern of the Soul, enlighten those whose minds are receptive:

> I shall set the light into the lantern and for all those whose eyes look on the light a special ray shall shine from the light into the eye of their knowledge. (III, 12, 11–13)

The polemical use of the eyes of the soul

In Book VI of the *FL* the topos of 'the eyes of the soul' acquires a particularly polemical edge when Mechthild deploys it in her reply to criticism that had been levelled at two of her earlier chapters (I, 44 and II, 4). The metaphor of the 'eyes of the soul' occurs most frequently in the context of visionary accounts and focuses attention on the knowledge Mechthild acquires through visions. However, in those chapters that have mystical union as their focus a vital link is established between love and knowledge.[21] Divine knowledge is the fruit of love and is granted to the soul in the ecstatic state of a personal encounter with God. This is expressed, for example, in that paradigmatic chapter of Book I where the path of the loving soul to mystical union with the Godhead is described:

> Then the Young Man comes to her and says: 'Young Lady, you should dance, following faithfully the steps my chosen ones have demonstrated to you.' Then she says: 'I cannot dance, Lord, unless You lead me. If You want me to dance with spring in my step, then You must lead me in with Your singing; then I shall spring into love, from love into knowledge, from knowledge into pleasure, from pleasure into what is beyond all human senses. . . .' (I, 44 [p. 34])

A point Mechthild makes in this chapter about the relationship of the Godhead with mankind appears to have met with some criticism to which she replies in Book VI. Her defence rests on an insistence on the illumination and enlightenment that is granted to the eye of the loving soul:

> I said in a passage in this book that the Godhead is my Father by nature. You did not understand this and you said: 'Every-

---

21 Cf. Heimbach (1989: 20ff.); Schmidt (1985: 140).

thing that God has done with us is through grace not through nature.' You are right and I am right too. Now listen to an analogy: however wonderful a person's eyes are, they cannot see over a mile away. However acute a person's senses are, he cannot grasp abstract things except through faith and he gropes in the darkness like a blind person. The loving Soul, that loves everything that God loves and hates everything that God hates, has an eye that God has illumined; with it she sees into the eternal Godhead, how the Godhead has worked with its nature in the Soul. (VI, 31 [p. 115])

Mechthild concludes the chapter by asserting the primacy of love. True love is the prerequisite of authentic knowledge:[22] 'Now listen: What we know is all nothing, unless we love God properly in all things, as He Himself has created all things in proper love and has offered and taught us love' (VI, 31 [p. 116]).

Through the insistence on the eyes of her soul in the accounts of her visionary encounters, Mechthild's writings further acquire, by analogy, that unassailable authority and validity which is generally accorded to an eyewitness account of a historical event. In II, 4 Mechthild had reported a vision of John the Baptist celebrating Mass and giving her communion. From what Mechthild says in VI, 36 it would seem that her critics felt that her vision implied that a layman could celebrate Mass. Where earlier in her book (II, 26; IV, 2; V, 12) Mechthild had turned to God for advice and guidance on how to deal with criticism of her work, here she assumes responsibility herself for the content of her writings, defending herself vehemently.[23] In this chapter she spells out for her critics the fundamental premise underlying her knowledge and insight. She opens her defence with an authoritative statement: 'We cannot comprehend divine gifts with human senses' and commences an attack on her critics that is couched in terms of physical sight and spiritual insight: '. . . that is why people, whose spirit is not open to the invisible truth, sin against themselves.' She foregrounds once more the unequal relationship between the Soul and the Body, reminding her critics of the inadequacy of human speech in the face of the ineffable:

That John the Baptist sang the Mass for the poor maid was not a physical reality, it was a spiritual experience that only

---

22 In this Schmidt (1995: 349, n. 20) sees a similarity to the thought of William of St Thierry.

23 Poor (1994) traces in the *FL* a progressive negotiation for authority. Cf. also Hollywood (1995: 65).

the Soul saw, understood and delighted in; but the Body had nothing of this except what it could comprehend in its human senses through the nobility of the Soul; that is why the words must be couched in human terms. (VI, 36 [p. 116]).

Mechthild then launches an unreserved attack on her critic calling him a 'Pharisee'.

John the Baptist, she argues, was not a layman because he touched God as priests do in administering the Eucharist. Thus, she claims priestly status for John in a metaphorical sense and asserts the superior knowledge of the spiritual over the physical senses:

That which we can see with the eyes of the Body, can hear with the ears of the Body, can speak with the mouth of the Body, that is as unlike the truth revealed to the loving Soul as the light of the candle is to the bright sun. (VI, 36 [p. 116])

Mechthild concludes her impassioned defence by accusing her critics of a lack of insight, an accusation which recalls her earlier judgement on the 'blindly devout' (I, 2 [p. 29]): 'Was this a layman? Answer me this, o you blind; your lies and your hate will never be forgiven without punishment.' (VI, 36 [p. 117])

Conclusion

The *FL* is conceived both as a channel of communication for God and as a testimony of individual witness. The visionary content of the *FL* is an account of how, through the grace of God, events in salvation history, both past and future, are made accessible to Mechthild, as are locations and figures in the afterlife. In her writings the linearity of salvation history is fragmented in a kaleidoscopic juxtaposition of past, present and future in the present of Mechthild's existence. Furthermore, through her fleeting experiences of mystical union with the Godhead, the Soul is transported to a state of existence beyond time. Mechthild's book offers the reader a devotional window with sight of and insight into the Godhead and salvation history through, on the one hand, the spiritual eyes of her soul and, on the other, the historical eyes of a religious woman of the thirteenth century.

Select bibliography

As will be evident from the publication dates of the secondary literature listed below, the current lively interest in Mechthild's writings within the English-speaking world was kindled in the wake of feminist studies in the 1970s and 1980s. The significant progress made in the editing and translating of Mechthild's book during the 1990s has provided the reader who has knowledge of Middle High German with the tools to engage effectively and confidently with the text. Tobin has rendered the English speaker a further service in his chronological survey (1995a) of secondary literature on the *FL*, in which he identifies particular trends in the reception of Mechthild's writings in their historical context. His bibliography is comprehensive, though not exhaustive. It may be supplemented and complemented by the bibliographies of Lewis (1989) and Andersen (2000). As the following select bibliography has been compiled primarily with the non-German speaker in mind, there is inevitably a heavy bias towards work in English. However, it should be borne in mind that the greater part of the seminal work in Mechthild scholarship has appeared in German. Some of the pieces that have been most influential in determining the course of Mechthild scholarship are included here as signposts: on the narrative structure of the *FL* (Kasten 1995; Kemper 1979) and dialogue in particular (Grubmüller 1992; Haug 1984; Largier 1987; Tillmann 1933); on the use of genres in the *FL* (Hellgardt 1996; Mohr 1963; Ortmann 1992); on the imagery of mysticism in the *FL* (Lüers 1926/66; Michel 1986); on the *FL* as autobiography (Neumann 1954/64; Peters 1988); on the *FL* within the context of vernacular and Latin literary cultures (Becker 1951; Köbele 1993; Margetts 1977; Ortmann 1992; Palmer 1992); on Mechthild's visionary life (Bochsler 1997; Schmidt 1985; Tax 1979); on Mechthild's prophetic voice (Heimbach 1989) and her mystic voice (Haas 1972 and 1975; Heimbach-Steins 1995); on the theology of Mechthild's spiritual life (Heimbach 1989; Schmidt 1995); on the historical context of the beguines in the history of German mysticism (Grundmann 1935/77); and on Mechthild's place in the history of western Christian mysticism (Ruh 1993). The English-speaking newcomer to Mechthild's writings will find first points of orientation in Andersen (2000), McGinn (1998) and Tobin (1995a).

Primary Sources

Editions of *Das fließende Licht der Gottheit*

Offenbarungen der Schwester Mechthild von Magdeburg oder Das fließende Licht der Gottheit. 1869. Aus der einzigen Handschrift des Stiftes Einsiedeln. Ed. Gall Morel. Regensburg. Reprinted, Darmstadt: Wissenschaftliche Buch Gesellschaft, 1963, 1976, 1980.

Das fließende Licht der Gottheit. 2 vols. 1990, 1993. Nach der Einsiedler Handschrift in kritischem Vergleich mit der gesamten Überlieferung. Ed. Hans Neumann. Vol. 1: *Text* arranged by Gisela Vollmann-Profe. Vol. 2: *Untersuchungen,* supplemented and prepared for printing by Gisela Vollmann-Profe. (Münchener Texte und Untersuchungen zur deutschen Literatur des Mittelalters. Vols. 100–101.) Munich: Artemis.

Edition of the *Lux divinitatis*

Lux divinitatis fluens in corda veritatis. 1877. In *Revelationes Gertrudianae ac Mechtildianae. II. Sanctae Mechtildis virginis ordinis sancti Benedicti Liber specialis gratiae, accedit sororis Mechtildis ejusdem ordinis Lux divinitatis.* Opus ad codicum fidem nunc primum integre editum Solesmensium O.S.B. monachorum cura et opera. Poitiers/Paris: Oudin. 423–643 (645ff. = Book VII).

Translations of *Das fließende Licht der Gottheit* into English

The Revelations of Mechthild of Magdeburg (1210–1297) or The Flowing Light of the Godhead. 1953. Transl. Lucy Menzies. New York: Longman's, Green.

Flowing Light of the Divinity. 1991. Transl. Christiane Mesch Galvani. Edited, with an introduction, by Susan Clark. New York/London: Garland.

Mechthild of Magdeburg. The Flowing Light of the Godhead. 1998. Transl. and introduced by Frank Tobin. Preface by Margot Schmidt. Mahwah, New York: Paulist Press.

Translations of *Das fließende Licht der Gottheit* into modern German

Das fließende Licht der Gottheit. 1955. Transl., with an introduction, by Margot Schmidt. Einsiedeln/Zurich/Cologne: Benzinger.

'Ich tanze, wenn du mich führst': Ein Höhepunkt deutscher Mystik. 1988. Transl. (selected passages), with an introduction, by Margot Schmidt. Freiburg im Breisgau: Herder.

Mechthild von Magdeburg. Das fließende Licht der Gottheit. 1995.

Second, revised transl., with an introduction and commentary, by Margot Schmidt. Stuttgart-Bad Cannstatt: frommann-holzboog.

Anthologies in English with extracts from *Das fließende Licht der Gottheit*

Bowie, Fiona. 1989. *Beguine Spirituality. An Anthology.* Transl. Oliver Davies. London: SPCK.

Larrington, Carolyne. 1995. *Women and Writing in Medieval Europe: A Sourcebook.* London/New York: Routledge.

Petroff, Elizabeth A. 1986. *Medieval Women's Visionary Literature.* Oxford/New York: Oxford University Press.

Wilson, Katharina M. Ed. 1984. *Medieval Women Writers.* Manchester: Manchester University Press.

Other Primary Texts

Saint Augustine. 1991. *Confessions.* Transl. Henry Chadwick. Oxford/New York: Oxford University Press.

Jacques de Vitry and Thomas de Cantimpré. 1993. *Two Lives of Marie d'Oignies.* Transl. Margot King and Hugh Feiss. 3rd edition. Toronto: Peregrina Publishing.

Mechthild von Hackeborn. *Revelationes Gertrudianae ac Mechtild-ianae. II. Sanctae Mechtildis virginis ordinis sancti Benedicti Liber specialis gratiae, accedit sororis Mechtildis ejusdem ordinis Lux divinitatis.* Opus ad codicum fidem nunc primum integre editum Solesmensium O.S.B. monachorum cura et opera. Poitiers/Paris: Oudin. 1–422.

Rudolf von Biberach. 1969. *'Die siben strassen zu got'.* Hochale-mannische Übertragung nach der Handschrift Einsiedeln 278. Ed., with an introduction, by Margot Schmidt. (Spicilegium Bonaventur-ianum VI). Florence.

Secondary Sources

Abraham, Ruth A. D. 1980. 'Mechthild of Magdeburg's "Flowing Light of the Godhead"; An Autobiographical Realization of Spiritual Poverty'. Unpublished dissertation: Stanford University.

Ancelet-Hustache, Jeanne. 1926. *Mechtilde de Magdebourg (1207–1282): Étude de psychologie religieuse.* Paris: Champion.

Andersen, Elizabeth A. 2000. *The Voices of Mechthild von Magdeburg.* Oxford/Bern: Peter Lang.

Becker, Ernst. 1951. 'Beiträge zur lateinischen und deutschen

Überlieferung des fließenden Lichts der Gottheit.' Unpublished dissertation, Göttingen.

Beer, Frances. 1992. 'Mechthild of Magdeburg.' In her *Women and Mystical Experience in the Middle Ages*. Woodbridge: Boydell Press. 78–108.

Bochsler, Katharina. 1997. *'Ich han da inne ungehoertú ding gesehen". Die Jenseitsvisionen Mechthilds von Magdeburg in der Tradition der mittelalterlichen Visionsliteratur.* (Deutsche Literatur von den Anfängen bis 1700, 23.) Bern/Berlin/Frankfurt a. M./New York/Paris/Vienna: Peter Lang.

Bolton, Brenda. 1976. 'Mulieres Sanctae.' In *Women in Medieval Society*. Ed. S. M. Stuard. University of Pennsylvania Press. 141–58.

————. 1999. 'Thirteenth-Century Religious Women. Further Reflections on the Low Countries "Special Case".' In *New Trends in Feminine Spirituality. The Holy Women of Liège and their Impact.* Ed. Juliette Dor, Lesley Johnson and Jocelyn Wogan-Browne. (Medieval Women: Texts and Contexts, 2.) European Union: Brepols. 129–58.

Bynum, Caroline Walker. 1982. 'Women Mystics in the Thirteenth Century: The Case of the Nuns of Helfta." In her *Jesus as Mother: Studies in the Spirituality of the High Middle Ages*. Berkeley: University of California Press. 170–262.

————. 1984. 'Women Mystics and Eucharistic Devotion in the Thirteenth Century.' *Women's Studies* 11: 179–214. Also in *Fragmentation and Redemption. Essays in Gender and the Human Body in Medieval Religion*. New York: Zone Books, 1992. 119–50.

Clark, Susan L. 1985. ' "Ze Glicher Wis": Mechthild von Magdeburg and the Concept of Likeness.' In *The Worlds of Medieval Women: Creativity, Influence, Imagination*. Ed. Constance H. Berman, Charles W. Connell and Judith Rice Rothschild. Morgantown: West Virginia University Press. 41–50.

Davies, Oliver. 1991. 'Hildegard von Bingen, Mechthild of Magdeburg and the young Meister Eckhart.' *Internationale Zeitschrift für interdisziplinäre Mittelalterforschung* 4: 37–51.

————. 'Transformational Processes in the work of Julian of Norwich and Mechthild of Magdeburg.' In *The Medieval Mystical Tradition in England*. Ed. Marion Glasscoe. Cambridge: D. S. Brewer. 30–52.

De Letter, P. 1967. 'Revelations, Private'. In *New Catholic Encyclopedia*. Ed. Catholic University of America. New York: McGraw-Hill. Vol. 12: 446–8.

Demayo, Thomas B. 1999. 'Mechthild of Magdeburg's mystical eschatology.' *Journal of Medieval History* 25: 399–415.

Devlin, Dennis. 1984. 'Feminine Lay Piety in the High Middle Ages:

The Beguines.' In *Distant Echoes, Medieval Religious Women*. Ed. J. A. Nichols and L. Th. Shank. Kalamazoo. Vol. 1: 183–96.

Dronke, Peter. 1984. *Women Writers of the Middle Ages. A Critical Study of Texts from Perpetua (? 203) to Marguerite Porete (? 1310)*. Cambridge: Cambridge University Press.

———. 1994. *Verse with Prose. The Art and Scope of the Mixed Form*. Cambridge, Massachusetts/London: Harvard University Press.

Egres, Odo. 1981. 'Mechthilde von Magdeburg: The Flowing Light of God.' In *Cistercians in the Late Middle Ages*. Ed. R. Elder. (Studies in Medieval Cistercian History 6, *Cistercian Studies* 64.) Kalamazoo, Michigan. 19–37.

———. 1984. 'Mechthild von Magdeburg: Exile in a Foreign Land.' In *Goad and Nail*. Ed. R. Elder. *Cistercian Studies* 10: 133–47.

Finnegan, Mary J., O. P. 1991. *The Women of Helfta: Scholars and Mystics*. Athens/London: The University of Georgia Press.

Franklin, James C. 1978. *Mystical Transformations: The Imagery of Liquids in the Work of Mechthild von Magdeburg*. London: Associated University Presses.

Gooday, Frances. 1974. 'Mechthild of Magdeburg and Hadewijch of Antwerp: A Comparison.' *Ons geestlijk erf* 48: 305–62.

Grubmüller, Klaus. 1992. 'Sprechen und Schreiben: Das Beispiel Mechthild von Magdeburg.' In *Festschrift für Walter Haug und Burghart Wachinger*. Ed. Johannes Janota et al. Tübingen: Niemeyer. Vol. 1: 335–48.

Grundmann, Herbert. 1935/reprinted 1977. *Religiöse Bewegungen im Mittelalter: Untersuchungen über die geschichtlichen Zusammenhänge zwischen der Ketzerei, den Bettelorden und der religiösen Frauenbewegung im 12. und 13. Jahrhundert und über die geschichtlichen Grundlagen der deutschen Mystik*. (Historische Studien, 267.) Berlin. Reprinted Darmstadt: Wissenschaftliche Buchgesellschaft. 1996. *Religious Movements in the Middle Ages*. Transl. Steven Rowan. Notre Dame, Ind.: University of Notre Dame Press.

Haas, Alois. 1972. 'Mechthild von Magdeburg – Dichtung und Mystik.' *Amsterdamer Beiträge zur älteren Germanistik* 2: 105–56. Also in: 1979. *Sermo Mysticus: Studien zur Theologie und Sprache der deutschen Mystik*. Freiburg (Switzerland), 67–103.

———. 1975. 'Die Struktur der mystischen Erfahrung nach Mechthild von Magdeburg.' *Freiburger Zeitschrift für Philosophie und Theologie* 22: 3–34. Also in Haas. *Sermo Mysticus* (see Haas 1972). 104–35.

Haug, Walter. 1984. 'Das Gespräch mit dem unvergleichlichen Partner: Der mystische Dialog bei Mechthild von Magdeburg als Paradigma für eine personale Gesprächsstruktur.' In *Das Gespräch*. Ed. Karlheinz Stierle and Rainer Warning. (*Poetik und Hermeneutik*, 11.) Munich. 251–79.

Heimbach, Marianne. 1989. *'Der ungelehrte Mund' als Autorität. Mystische Erfahrung als Quelle kirchlich-prophetischer Rede im Werk Mechthilds von Magdeburg*. (Mystik in Geschichte und Gegenwart: Abteilung 1, Christliche Mystik, 6.) Stuttgart-Bad Cannstatt: frommann-holzboog.

Heimbach-Steins, Marianne. 1995. 'Gottes und des Menschen "heimlichkeit". Zu einem Zentralbegriff der mystischen Theologie Mechthilds von Magdeburg.' In *Contemplata aliis tradere. Studien zum Verhältnis von Literatur und Spiritualität*. Ed. Claudia Brinker et al. Bern/Berlin/Frankfurt a. M./New York/Paris/Vienna: Peter Lang. 71–86.

Hellgardt, Ernst. 1996. 'Darbietungsformen geistlicher Gehalte im Werk Mechthilds von Magdeburg.' In *Die Vermittlung geistlicher Inhalte im deutschen Mittelalter*. Internationales Symposium, Roscrea 1994. Ed. Timothy R. Jackson, Nigel F. Palmer and Almut Suerbaum. Tübingen: Niemeyer. 319–37.

Hollywood, Amy. 1995. *The Soul as Virgin Wife. Mechthild of Magdeburg, Marguerite Porete and Meister Eckhart*. Notre Dame, Ind.: University of Notre Dame Press.

Howard, John. 1984. 'The German Mystic: Mechthild of Magdeburg.' In *Medieval Women Writers*. Ed. Katharina M. Wilson. Manchester: Manchester University Press. 153–85.

Kasten, Ingrid. 1995. 'Formen des Narrativen in Mechthilds *Fließendem Licht der Gottheit*.' In *Contemplata aliis tradere. Studien zum Verhältnis von Literatur und Spiritualität*. Ed. Claudia Brinker et al. Bern/Berlin/Frankfurt a. M./New York/Paris/Vienna: Peter Lang.

Kemper, Hans-Georg. 1979. 'Allegorische Allegorese: Zur Bildlichkeit und Struktur mystischer Literatur.' In *Formen und Funktionen der Allegorie*. Symposium Wolfenbüttel, 1978. Ed. Walter Haug. (Germanistische Symposien, 3) Stuttgart. 90–125.

Köbele, Susanne. 1993. *Bilder der unbegriffenen Wahrheit. Zur Struktur mystischer Rede im Spannungsfeld von Latein und Volkssprache*. (Bibliotheca Germanica, 30.) Tübingen/Basle: Francke. 32–39; 71–96.

Largier, Niklaus. 1987. 'Anima mea liquefacta est. Der Dialog der Seele mit Gott bei Mechthild von Magdeburg und Heinrich Seuse.' *Internationale Katholische Zeitschrift* 16: 227–32.

Lewis, Gertrud Jaron. 1989. *Bibliographie zur deutschen Frauenmystik des Mittelalters*. With an appendix on Beatrijs van Nazareth and

Hadewijch by Frank Willaert and Marie-José Govers. (Bibliographien zur deutschen Literatur des Mittelalters, 10.) Berlin: Erich Schmidt.

Lüers, Grete. 1926/reprinted 1966. *Die Sprache der deutschen Mystik des Mittelalters im Werke der Mechthild von Magdeburg*. Munich: Ernst Reinhardt/reprinted Darmstadt: Wissenschaftliche Buchgesellschaft.

Margetts, John. 1977. 'Latein und Volkssprache bei Mechthild von Magdeburg.' *Amsterdamer Beiträge zur älteren Germanistik* 12: 119–36.

McDonnell, E. W. 1954/reprinted 1969. *The Beguines and Beghards in Medieval Culture with Special Emphasis on the Belgian Scene*. New Brunswick, N.J.: Rutgers University Press/reprinted New York: Octagon Books.

McGinn, Bernard. 1998. 'Mechthild of Magdeburg.' In his *The Presence of God: A History of Western Christian Mysticism*. Vol. III. The Flowering of Mysticism. Men and Women in the New Mysticism (1200–1350). New York: Crossroad. 222–44.

——. 1999. 'Suffering, emptiness and annihilation in three beguine mystics.' In *Homo Medietas: Aufsätze zu Religiosität, Literatur und Mentalität des Menschen vom Mittelalter bis in die Neuzeit*. Festschrift für Alois Maria Haas zum 65. Geburtstag. Ed. Claudia Brinker-von der Heyde and Niklaus Largier. Bern/Frankfurt a. M.: Peter Lang. 155–74.

Michel, Paul. 1986. 'Durch die bilde über die bilde: Zur Bildgestaltung bei Mechthild von Magdeburg.' In *Abendländische Mystik im Mittelalter*. Symposion Kloster Engelberg. Ed. Kurt Ruh. Stuttgart: Metzler. 509–26.

Mohr, Wolfgang. 1963. 'Darbietungsformen der Mystik bei Mechthild von Magdeburg.' In *Märchen, Mythos, Dichtung: Festschrift zum 90. Geburtstag Friedrich von der Leyens*. Ed. Hugo Kuhn und Kurt Schier. Munich: Beck. 375–99.

Murk-Jansen, Saskia. 1998. *Brides in the Desert. The Spirituality of the Beguines*. London: Dartman, Longman and Todd Ltd.

Nellmann, Eberhard. 1989. ' "Dis buoch . . . bezeichent alleine mich." Zum Prolog von Mechthilds "Fließenden Licht der Gottheit." ' In *Gotes und der werlde hulde: Literatur in Mittelalter und Neuzeit*. Festschrift für Heinz Rupp zum 70. Geburtstag. Ed. Rüdiger Schnell. Bern/Stuttgart: Francke. 206–23.

Neumann, Hans 1954. 'Beiträge zur Textgeschichte des "Fließenden Lichts der Gottheit" und zur Lebensgeschichte Mechthilds von Magdeburg.' *Nachrichten der Akademie der Wissenschaften in*

Göttingen. Phil.-hist. Klasse, Jg. 1954, Nr. 3: 27–80. Quoted from the abbreviated and corrected version (1964) in *Altdeutsche und altniederländische Mystik*. Ed. Kurt Ruh. Darmstadt: Wissenschaftliche Buchgesellschaft. 175–239.

———. 1987. 'Mechthild von Magdeburg.' In *Die deutsche Literatur des Mittelalters: Verfasserlexikon*. Ed. Kurt Ruh together with Gundolf Keil et al. Berlin/New York: Walter de Gruyter. Vol. 6: Cols. 260–70.

Ortmann, Christa. 1992. 'Das Buch der Minne. Methodologischer Versuch zur deutsch-lateinischen Gegebenheit des "Fließenden Lichts der Gottheit" Mechthilds von Magdeburg.' In *Grundlagen des Verstehens mittelalterlicher Literatur. Literarische Texte und ihr historischer Erkenntniswert*. Ed. Gerhard Hahn and Hedda Ragotzky. (Kröners Studienbibliothek, 663.) Stuttgart: Kröner. 158–86.

Palmer, Nigel F. 1992. 'Das Buch als Bedeutungsträger bei Mechthild von Magdeburg.' In *Bildhafte Rede in Mittelalter und früher Neuzeit: Probleme ihrer Legitimation und Funktion*. Ed. Wolfgang Harms and Klaus Speckenbach. Tübingen: Niemeyer. 217–35.

Peters, Ursula. 1988. *Religiöse Erfahrung als literarisches Faktum: Zur Vorgeschichte und Genese frauenmystischer Texte des 13. und 14. Jahrhunderts*. Tübingen: Niemeyer.

Poor, Sara S. 1994. 'Medieval Incarnation of Self: Subjectivity and Authority in the Writings of Mechthild von Magdeburg.' Unpublished dissertation, Duke University.

———. 1999. 'Gender und Autorität in der Konstruktion einer schriftlichen Tradition.' In *Autorität der/in Sprache, Literatur, Neuen Medien*. Vorträge des Bonner Germanistentages 1997. Ed. Jürgen Fohrmann, Ingrid Kasten and Eva Neuland. Bielefeld: Aisthesis. Vol. 2: 532–52.

———. 2000a. 'Historicizing Canonicity: Tradition and the Invisible Talent of Mechthild von Magdeburg.' *Women in German Yearbook* 15: 49–72.

———. 2000b. 'Cloaking the Body in Text: the Question of Female Authorship in the Writings of Mechthild von Magdeburg.' *Exemplaria* 12: 417–53.

Ruh, Kurt. 1993. *Geschichte der abendländischen Mystik*. Vol. II: Frauenmystik und franziskanische Mystik der Frühzeit. Munich: Beck.

Schmidt, Margot. 1982. 'Die Augensymbolik bei Ephräm und Parallelen in der deutschen Mystik.' In *Typus, Symbol, Allegorie bei den östlichen Vätern und ihren Parallelen im Mittelalter*. Ed. Margot

Schmidt with C. F. Geyer. (Eichstätter Beiträge, 4.) Regensburg. 278–301.

―――. 1984. 'Das Auge als Symbol der Erleuchtung bei Ephräm und Parallelen in der Mystik des Mittelalters.' *Oriens Christianus* 68: 27–57.

―――. 1985. 'Elemente der Schau bei Mechthild von Magdeburg und Mechthild von Hackeborn: Zur Bedeutung der geistlichen Sinne.' In *Frauenmystik im Mittelalter.* Ed. Peter Dinzelbacher and Dieter R. Bauer. Ostfildern bei Stuttgart. 123–51.

―――. 1987. 'Minne dü gewaltige kellerin. On the nature of *Minne* in Mechthild's *Fließendes Licht der Gottheit.*' *Vox benedictina* 4: 100–25.

―――. 1998. 'The importance of Christ in the correspondence between Jordan of Saxony and Diana d'Andalo, and in the writings of Mechthild of Magdeburg.' In *Christ among the Medieval Dominicans: Representations of Christ in the Texts and Images of the Order of Preachers.* Ed. Kent Emery, Jr. and Joseph Wawrykow. (Notre Dame Conferences in Medieval Sudies, 7.) Notre Dame, Ind.: University of Notre Dame Press. 100–12.

Scholl, Edith. 1984. 'To be a Full-Grown Bride: Mechthild of Magdeburg.' In *Medieval Religious Women.* II. *Peace Weavers.* Ed. J. A. Nichols and L. Th. Shank. (Cistercian Studies Series, 72.) Kalamazoo, MI: Cistercian Publications. 223–37.

Schulze-Belli, Paola. 1999. 'A new perspective on the metaphorical language of Mechthild von Magdeburg's *Flowing Light of the Godhead.* Some considerations about the language of the mystics.' *Jahrbuch der Oswald von Wolkenstein-Gesellschaft* 11: 211–32.

Seaton, William. 1984. 'Transforming of Convention in Mechthild of Magdeburg.' *Mystics Quarterly* 10: 64–72.

Shahar, Shulamith. 1983. *The Fourth Estate. A History of Women in the Middle Ages.* Transl. Chaya Galai. London/New York: Routledge.

Sinka, Margit. 1985. 'Christological Mysticism in Mechthild von Magdeburg's *Das fließende Licht der Gottheit*: A Journey of Wounds.' *Germanic Review* 60: 123–8.

Stoudt, Debra L. 1991. ' "Ich súndig wip muos schriben": Religious Woman and Literary Traditions.' In *Women as Protagonists and Poets in the German Middle Ages. An Anthology of Feminist Approaches to Middle High German Literature.* Ed. Albrecht Classen. (Göppinger Arbeiten zur Germanistik, 528.) Göppingen: Kümmerle. 147–68.

Strauch, Gabriele L. 1991. 'Mechthild von Magdeburg and the Category of Frauenmystik.' In *Women as Protagonists and Poets in the German Middle Ages. An Anthology of Feminist Approaches to*

Middle High German Literature. Ed. Albrecht Classen. (Göppinger Arbeiten zur Germanistik, 528.) Göppingen: Kümmerle. 171–86.

Tax, Petrus W. 1979. 'Die große Himmelsschau Mechthilds von Magdeburg und ihre Höllenvision.' *Zeitschrift für deutsches Altertum und deutsche Literatur* 108: 112–37.

Tillmann, Heinz. 1933. *Studien zum Dialog bei Mechthild von Magdeburg.* Marburg: Kalbfleisch.

Tobin, Frank. 1994. 'Mechthild of Magdeburg and Meister Eckhart: Points of Comparison.' In *Meister Eckhart and the Beguine Mystics. Hadewijch of Brabant, Mechthild of Magdeburg and Marguerite Porete.* Ed. Bernard McGinn. New York: Continuum. 44–61.

———. 1995a. *Mechthild von Magdeburg. A Medieval Mystic in Modern Eyes.* Columbia: Camden House.

———. 1995b. 'Medieval Thought on Visions and Its Resonance in Mechthild von Magdeburg's *Flowing Light of the Godhead.*' In *Vox Mystica. Essays for Valerie M. Lagorio.* Ed. Anne Clark Bartlett et al. Cambridge: D. S. Brewer. 41–53.

Voaden, Rosalynn. 1995. 'God's Almighty Hand: Women Co-Writing the Book.' In *Women, the Book and the Godly.* Selected proceedings of the St Hilda's Conference, 1993. Vol. 1. Ed. Lesley Smith and Jane H. M. Taylor. Cambridge: D. S. Brewer. 55–66.

———. 1996. 'Women's words, men's language: *Discretio spirituum* as discourse in the writing of women visionaries.' *The Medieval Translator* 5: 64–83.

Wiethaus, Ulrike. 1986. 'The Reality of Mystical Experience: Self and World in the Work of Mechthild of Magdeburg.' Unpublished dissertation, Temple University.

———. 1996. *Ecstatic Transformation. Transpersonal Psychology in the Work of Mechthild of Magdeburg.* Syracuse, New York: Syracuse University Press.

Wright, T. R. 1988. *Theology and Literature* (Signposts in Theology.) Oxford: Blackwell.

Index

Already published titles in this series

Christine de Pizan's Letter of Othea to Hector, *Jane Chance*, 1990

The Writings of Margaret of Oingt, Medieval Prioress and Mystic, *Renate Blumenfeld-Kosinski*, 1990

Saint Bride and her Book: Birgitta of Sweden's Revelations, *Julia Bolton Holloway*, 1992

The Memoirs of Helene Kottanner (1439–1440), *Maya Bijvoet Williamson*, 1998

The Writings of Teresa de Cartagena, *Dayle Seidenspinner-Núñez*, 1998

Julian of Norwich: *Revelations of Divine Love* and *The Motherhood of God*: an excerpt, *Frances Beer*, 1998

Hrotsvit of Gandersheim: A Florilegium of her Works, *Katharina M. Wilson*, 1998

Hildegard of Bingen: On Natural Philosophy and Medicine: Selections from *Cause et Cure, Margret Berger*, 1999

Women Saints' Lives in Old English Prose, *Leslie A. Donovan*, 1999

Angela of Foligno's Memorial, *Cristina Mazzoni*, 2000

The Letters of the Rožmberk Sisters, *John M. Klassen*, 2001

The Life of Saint Douceline, a Beguine of Provence, *Kathleen Garay and Madeleine Jeay*, 2001

Agnes Blannbekin, Viennese Beguine: Life and Revelations, *Ulrike Wiethaus*, 2002

Women of the *Gilte Legende*: A Selection of Middle English Saints Lives, *Larissa Tracy*, 2003

The Book of Margery Kempe: An Abridged Translation, *Liz Herbert McAvoy*, 2003

Mechthild of Magdeburg: Selections from *The Flowing Light of the Godhead*, *Elizabeth A. Andersen*, 2003

Guidance for Women in Twelfth-Century Convents, *Vera Morton with Jocelyn Wogan-Browne*, 2003

Goscelin of St Bertin: *The Book of Encouragement and Consolation [Liber Confortatorius]*, *Monika Otter*, 2004

Anne of France: *Lessons for my Daughter*, *Sharon L. Jansen*, 2004

Late-Medieval German Women's Poetry: Secular and Religious Songs, *Albrecht Classen*, 2004

The Paston Women: Selected Letters, *Diane Watt*, 2004

The Vision of Christine de Pizan, Glenda McLeod and Charity Cannon Willard, 2005

Caritas Pirckheimer: A Journal of the Reformation Years, 1524-1528, *Paul A. McKenzie*, 2006

Women's Books of Hours in Medieval England, *Charity Scott-Stokes*, 2006

Old Norse Women's Poetry: The Voices of Female Skalds, *Sandra Ballif Straubhaar*, 2011